Let It Go

Let It Go

*Forgive So You
Can Be Forgiven*

T.D. Jakes

ATRIA PAPERBACK
New York   London   Toronto   Sydney   New Delhi

ATRIA PAPERBACK
A Division of Simon & Schuster, Inc.
1230 Avenue of the Americas
New York, NY 10020

First Atria Paperback edition January 2013

ATRIA PAPERBACK and colophon are trademarks of Simon & Schuster, Inc.

For information about special discounts for bulk purchases, please contact Simon & Schuster Special Sales at 1-866-506-1949 or business@simonandschuster.com.

The Simon & Schuster Speakers Bureau can bring authors to your live event. For more information or to book an event, contact the Simon & Schuster Speakers Bureau at 1-866-248-3049 or visit our website at www.simonspeakers.com.

Manufactured in the United States of America

20 19 18 17 16 15 14

The Library of Congress has cataloged the hardcover edition as follows:

Jakes, T.D.
    Let it go : forgive so you can be forgiven / T.D. Jakes. — 1st Atria Books hardcover ed.
        p.   cm.
    1. Forgiveness—Biblical teaching.   2. Christian life.   I. Title.
    BJ1476.J344   2012
    234'.5—dc23   2011047957

ISBN 978-1-4165-4729-7
ISBN 978-1-4165-4733-4 (pbk)
ISBN 978-1-4391-7714-3 (ebook)

I dedicate this book to all of the men and women who carry around burdens of unforgiveness for the many trials, transgressions, and trespasses in their lives. I pray that you may find strength, comfort, and hope within these pages, and, through the power of forgiveness, be released from the crushing weight on your shoulders.

Contents

Let It Go

Introduction:
The Reason Why

'm always amazed at family reunions at the people who say, "Why, you haven't changed a bit!" It's usually said by a great-aunt sipping iced tea on the front porch or a cousin who blindsides you near the chips and dip, or some distant relative from your grandfather's side of the family whom you haven't seen since you had pimples and braces. It used to annoy me, as if they couldn't see how much I'd grown, matured, developed, and changed.

As if they couldn't tell how much better I had become—more successful, more influential, more important. Not to mention more humble! I'm no longer that stocky little boy sitting thoughtfully on grandma's rocking chair, listening to the adults reminisce about the good old days and gossip about what cousin Lucy is wearing. I'm a grown man who leads an international ministry and travels around the world and writes books and makes movies.

It seems so clear to those relatives, as if they can see the consistent pieces within both the boy and the man. Yet when I think about who I was as a child, my memories of boyhood incidents do not always seem to reflect the man I became. Certainly, there are a few events that reflect my adult self when I view them through this lens. I remember finding a litter of nine puppies while on the way home from my paper route when I was probably nine or ten years old. Their mother's lifeless body lay in a ditch, a casualty of a speeding car along that busy highway.

The cries of the newborn pups from the nearby bushes alerted me to their defenseless state and insistent hunger. It didn't even occur to me to leave them lying there, whimpering for the mother who would never return to nurse them. Taking them home nestled in my empty newspaper carrier, I placed an old towel in the bottom of a cardboard box for them and then proceeded to come up with a plan to alleviate their hunger.

I emptied a Palmolive dishwashing liquid bottle and filled it with warm milk mixed with a little oatmeal (I have no idea why I added this—maybe it was the closest ingredient at hand that reminded me of baby food!). Using the squeeze dispenser cap, I nursed each puppy and managed to keep them alive this way for several days until they could be placed with new owners in loving homes.

I must tell you, though, that I wished I had saved that liquid soap that I poured out in order to use the squeeze bottle. I could have used it to clean the enormous mess made by those puppies the next morning. Because something I learned about feeding puppies with milk and oatmeal is that it produces diarrhea! Talk about unbearable! I thought my mother was going to drop *me* in a ditch somewhere when she saw the huge mess my new responsibilities had made—on the porch, in the garage, and all over our yard.

Rooting for the Underdogs

"What does this incident have to do with the man I have become?" you might ask. While I'm certainly not a veterinarian or dog trainer now, there's something about the plight of these orphaned pups that pulled at my heartstrings so powerfully that I could not resist helping them, nurturing them, and finding a way for them not only to survive but thrive. I didn't help them out of a sense of moral obligation or a guilt-triggered feeling of having to do the right thing. No, I was clearly supposed to find them and perform the joyful privilege of offering what I had to give.

Reflecting on this memory as a microcosm of what I do in my life now, I am still drawn by the challenge of caring for the underdogs, those people who are at the end of their rope and at the bottom of the barrel, individuals who may appear to have everything but are emotionally orphaned inside, secretly feeling just as helpless as those puppies. People whom others have given up on and who may want to give up on themselves. I'm not Superman and certainly do not have a Messiah complex, as the clinicians label people who must save others in order to feel good about themselves. I simply have an awareness of my purpose that dates back to a time when caring for a litter of helpless puppies was as natural to me as breathing.

Over the past thirty-five years, I've spent my life interacting with an amazing diversity of people around the world. I've been privileged to pray with tribesmen in the African bush, address children in New Zealand, and sing gospel hymns with women in prison. I've continually been blessed by these encounters and received more than I think I gave them, learning to appreciate that we are all more alike than different, more full of light than darkness, more full of love than violence.

However, we don't always see ourselves the way others are able to see into us, whether they be relatives or not. I believe we often fail to make the connections between where we started on our journey and the place where we currently find ourselves. My hope is that this book will help you gain insight into what prevents you from being the husband you want to be, the wife you long to be, the mother or father you know is inside you, the creative person you were born to be—the most successful version of you possible! The following pages will change your life if you take my message to heart. And it won't be easy! I'm not suggesting methods for trimming the hedges of your behavior but for getting to the bitter roots of the issues that consistently strangle your potential. But it will be more than worth the effort to free yourself from a burden that's been crippling you for far too long.

End the Masquerade

Psychologists, doctors, and researchers tell us that our personalities are clearly formed and defined even as toddlers. Studies indicate that by the time we're in third grade, most of our inner motivations, coping skills, and personal preferences have been established. Before we even get close to the teenaged years, we have become most of who we are to become.

In most cases, we develop a defensive strategy in our formative years that we will wear like a mask through the rest of our life. We begin repeating this cycle of responding to experiences in certain ways and then have it reinforced by the traumas of life—death, divorce, betrayal, loss, renewal. No doubt, our personalities incline us toward relating to the world in particular ways. Very quickly we learn what works and what doesn't work, how to get attention and how to avoid it, when to speak up and when to remain silent.

Simply put, we encounter life and learn that it does not indeed revolve around us.

We are forced to learn to accommodate life on its own terms. We may be blessed with loving parents in an affluent household, but we must still face getting cut from the team, making the bad grade, being rejected by the cute girl at the dance. Or we may have grown up in an impoverished, abusive home and worked hard for good grades for a scholarship out of our circumstances. In either case, we became conditioned to expect life to work a certain way as well as conditioned to interact with those around us in particular ways.

In short, we learn that life is not fair, that it doesn't yield to our wishes, and that faith without a lot of hard work can be excruciatingly disappointing. We learn the street lessons that you cannot learn in the classroom, the educational tools that must be acquired in the alleys of altercation and tunnels of treachery. If we don't defend ourselves, we will be run over. If we don't ask for what we want and take it, no one will read our mind and give it to us. If we don't fight for ourselves, then we're afraid we'll never get ahead.

Consequently, each of us learns, adapts, and adjusts to facing life in the wake of our personal disappointments, private losses, and public fiascoes. Soon this style of relating becomes that garment of its own making, shielding us from the bitter winds and glaring stares of others while insulating our hearts from the chill that can come from an unexpected storm. Often, however, this garment is outdated and no longer serves its original purpose, becoming a ragged bandage for this part of ourselves where our deepest fears and harshest hurts reside.

Left unattended, ignored, or neglected, this part of us, like any wound, is prone to infection. We may be functioning well enough, even achieving and succeeding; however, this part of ourselves throbs and aches and reminds us of what has damaged us in the past. In order to experience the glow of full health and wholeness, we need some way to heal this hurt, wounded, damaged, injured, infected part of ourselves; otherwise, the infection grows and slowly, gradually continues to debilitate all areas of our lives.

Whether we realize it or not, our infection infiltrates our gifts, our talents, our workplace, our relationships, every aspect and area of our lives. Just as an internal infection can go septic and poison our blood, which then spreads throughout our body, so can this personal and emotional infection spread and affect all areas of our life—our ability to interact with coworkers, to make new friends, to ask someone out on a date, etc.

The mask that was once our protection, our shield hiding a personal wound against further trauma, often evolves into a cumbersome shroud smothering the life out of us. We end up overreacting to the negative criticisms of others, reading messages into their input that they never intended. We feel caught in a masquerade of our own making to the point that we no longer are sure who we really are. If we don't find ways to effectively process the toxicity of our past traumas, then we not only jeopardize our own well-being, but we risk infecting the next generations with the same germs of dis-ease.

Don't Drink the Water

I remember as a child talking nonstop as my mother sat across from me and listened attentively. I have no idea what I went on and on about—probably the typical childish stories of what happened at school that day, what I learned in geography class, or who I played with at recess. But my mother always listened and made me feel important. She would turn from folding laundry to look me in the eye and show me she was listening to my heart.

When I asked her years later if she remembered those times, she said, "Yes, absolutely. I wanted to hear every word you had to say, not because it was so incredibly important, but because I wanted you to know you were incredibly important. When you give a child your attention, you let them know that their ideas are valuable. When you ignore what a child says, you devalue that child and teach him that what he thinks doesn't matter to anyone."

Research studies have shown that many people become more introverted in their personalities as a coping mechanism resulting from the relational assaults of childhood. It doesn't necessarily have to be abuse or neglect that precipitates such a relational style; it can simply be a sensitive child picking up on the troubled emotions of those around her. The emotional load becomes too much for the child to bear, and she has to go within and secure herself within her own thoughts, ideas, and emotions. The child feels drained and cannot process the ongoing psychological and emotional load that she has taken upon herself.

I believe everyone does this to some extent. Parents are pulled in every direction, so busy with the demands of keeping food on the table and a roof over everyone, and often unintentionally send mixed messages to their children. They tell their children they love them but then do not have time to sit down and hear about the book report, the basketball tryouts, or the cute boy who might ask her to the dance. We want relationship and long to love and be loved, and yet we all experience the painful disappointment of rejection, abandonment, or betrayal.

As we move into adulthood, our desires for human relationship mature and deepen even as our life experiences teach us that loving others is risky business, often resulting in hurt feelings, painful misunderstandings, and unexpected disappointments. We become cynical and skeptical, often without even realizing it. Bitterness leaches into the groundwater of our soul, slowly permeating our entire being. We don't learn how to advance through it, how to filter out the sediments and foreign matters that block and poison us when left unimpeded.

It's not wrong or bad or evil to have this problem; it's simply human. You are just misunderstood. However, carrying this impediment around eventually infiltrates all that you do. "Welcome to JCPenney—how may I help you?" reveals it, "Would you like to have dinner with me this weekend?" displays it, and "You may not stay out past curfew, young lady!" illustrates it. We may be totally unaware of the silent, unmistakable message we are sending with our eyes, our voice, our body language, our mannerisms, our attitude and intonation, but it's there and it's loud and clear to those around us—our customers, our coworkers, our spouses and children.

Jesus once asked his disciples, "Who do people say that I am?" After collecting the local headlines of public opinion, he then asked his twelve followers, "Who do you say that I am?" Eleven of them said nothing at all! They had left their jobs, their families, their former lives to follow this man claiming to be the Son of God, and yet all but one of them could not say who they really thought he was. Often after years of deep investment into others we are shocked and disappointed that they simply didn't get who we really are. We soon learn that not only do we bring pollutants into our relationships that affect how we perceive and are being perceived, but those around us have their own pollution. We all may be doing and saying the right things, but beneath the surface, our individual needs, fears, and motives seep out between the lines of our words and deeds and even our silence, providing only ambiguity when life demands a definitive answer.

Foreign Matters

All of this debris, all the little pieces and particles of these foreign matters, clings to us like a layer of smoke. You don't even have to smoke to be around someone who does and absorb a fine, thin film of smoke in your clothes, skin, and hair. You may not even notice it anymore, but others do as soon as you enter the room.

My doctor told me at one point that I had a virus in my body that sometimes causes me to be fatigued and exhausted, similar to mononucleosis. I asked my doctor how I acquired such a virus, and he told me that it likely originated simply from my exposure to huge numbers of people. We develop a similar condition based on our exposure to the vast number of people throughout our lives. We are vulnerable to the hurts, heartaches, and disappointments that result from virtually any human interaction.

Your heart says love, your mouth wants to articulate the same message, but somewhere between your heart and your tongue, foreign matters affect not only what you say, but how you say it, or whether you respond at all. Foreign matters become formative matters, which results in misunderstanding. You know the feeling. You're alone in a crowd, married and yet still feeling single, attached and yet detached from life. The problem is so pervasive.

We learn to risk by making deposits into relationships with other people. Based on the deposits, we then determine whether to proceed with an investment of our time, attention, and heart space. As we encounter people who let us down, people who say one thing and do another, people who promise more than they deliver, we learn to make very limited deposits and to limit true investments altogether.

However, in order to succeed, life demands full investments. When our bodies are infected, doctors will wait until the infection has been arrested and eradicated before attempting surgery or some other corrective procedure. Similarly, we must stop the spread of our malaise at its origin; otherwise, the cycle will continually replay itself over and over in an endless loop of the same old song.

So often we know what we would like to do and yet we never feel up to what is required to make forward progress. We can't seem to muster the strength to go back to school, to go on a date, to allow ourselves to fall in love, to become parents, to start a new business. I want you to find your best self. Success is always intentional. No one walks across the stage to accept a college degree by accident. No one crosses the finish line in a marathon because they got lost in the woods. No one who succeeds wakes up one day and asks, "Where am I? How did I get here?"

A partial deposit does not yield the kind of results necessary to succeed in life. Foreign matters limit our ability to invest with healthy, sustainable deposits. We end up stuck in place, forever on a treadmill, wondering why we don't make progress whenever we try and run faster. Foreign matters shut you down. They drain your energy, your creativity, your productivity, your ability to imagine your life differently. They severely limit your ability to fulfill your God-given potential.

It's like a car with eight cylinders going up a hill. You don't have full power of all eight cylinders and instead must sputter and struggle on the few that are firing to keep going up the incline. You can't bring your full energy to the task at hand, you can't climb the hill before you any given day without an exhaustive expulsion of your very limited resources. With our bodies, we know that we must eat properly and exercise regularly if we are to expect our bodies to perform under stress, whether it be a marathon or simply hoops with the kids in the driveway before dinner.

If we know that our cars and our bodies require proper maintenance to perform at peak levels, then why would we expect any less from our personality? Too often we are simply not capable of bringing our full self to the table. We're only bringing a limited amount of our true capabilities. The people around us are only seeing 60 percent or 40 percent or 25 percent of who we really are and what we're truly capable of achieving. It's like a heart with a blocked artery that can only allow 20 percent of the body's blood supply to be oxygenated and pumped throughout the rest of the body. We're forced to get by on this limited supply and wonder why we gasp for air as we take more than a few steps.

You deserve to live your life at 100 percent. You are entitled to bring your full self to the task. This current season of your life could truly be your greatest. You could finally be operating on a full tank, fueling your dreams with all eight cylinders running at full speed, all pistons firing with new points and plugs!

Rehabilitating Hope

Where do we begin? I'm so glad you asked, because the catalyst is to do what you just did—ask the right questions. So often we're told not to question, especially questions related to our faith and the ways of God. Yet if students are not allowed to question, then how are they expected to learn? Without allowing questions, students are denied the opportunity to learn for themselves, to own and utilize inquiry as an educational tool.

We see this in the development of children. Beginning around the "terrible twos," children ask question after question, usually resulting in a litany of "why?" after "why?" "Why do I have to take a nap, Mommy?" "Well, so you can get the rest your body needs to grow big and strong." "Why does my body need rest to get big and strong?" "Well, so you can regain energy from all that playing you were doing this morning." "Why did I lose energy when I was playing this morning?" If you're a parent, then you know the drill! The one that can feel like endless torture with a toddler-sized attorney taking a deposition on the fundamentals of daily functioning!

Ask yourself, "How did I get to this point in my life? Is this where I want to go? Where I thought I was going? Am I really living the life I was meant to live? Am I satisfied with the quality and quantity of relationships in my life?" I challenge you to make an honest assessment of what you're carrying at this moment. I encourage you to lay it down and let it go.

I'm not sure why the eleven disciples didn't really get who Jesus was, but there could be a reason why people don't get you. You're not a bad person. You're a good person with a loving heart. There's nothing wrong with you that cannot be changed. Your lifelong infection puts them off, impedes their response to you. You have not gotten where you should have gotten. This infection is very likely the reason why.

Most people are not very self-aware; they have not been conditioned to know themselves. And if we're not aware of all the negative debris washing under the bridge of our hearts, then how much harder it can be to hope for real change. A recent article in the Trinity Forum on faith, churches, criminals, and change offered a simple, but not simplistic, prescriptive admonition: more God, less crime, more attention to character formation and more hope in character reformation. The article asserted that being incarcer-

ated is never a neutral experience and tends to exploit and reinforce the weaknesses of character that brought the inmate there
in the first place.

It's very difficult once certain patterns are established to
change our conditioned default settings. Many of us wonder if
true change is possible for those incarcerated and yet if we're honest, we must ask ourselves the same question. We have all had incidents and altercations, accidents and inhibitions that have left
us scarred, calloused, and unsteady on our feet. We become unwit-
ting saboteurs of our own destiny, imprisoning ourselves to a life
sentence of mediocrity.

We are predisposed to perceive and to respond to the events in
our life based on early conditioning and repetitive reinforcement.
If you act like you will never succeed, then others will see you as
someone who doesn't have what it takes. If you project an air of
bitterness based on the harsh criticism of your childhood, then
others will avoid you in order to sidestep the caustic atmosphere
hovering around you.

Birthrights

Jesus says that unless you become as little children you will not
inherit the kingdom of God. Now, keep in mind, he's saying this to
grown men. Here he tells us that we must return to the beginning,
go back to our roots, and start again. To get back on the road of
our divinely intended destiny, we must let go of the debris, clear
the clutter, and begin again with a clean sheet, seeking the intui-
tive wisdom of the childlike origination from which we grew.

It seems a difficult task and leaves us asking as adults how a
man, when he is old, can go back to his mother's womb, yet that
is precisely what Jesus recommends. To dare to take the risk of

living, of loving, of believing, with childlike simplicity of faith, to bring your full self into every present moment, to go from making halfhearted deposits into making the investment of a life worth living. As we let go of the debris, the emotional detritus that has clogged our valves and prevented our functioning at full capacity, we will rediscover ourselves, our best selves, and at that point, all those around us will reap the reward of the kind of investments that separate challengers from champions.

I will admit that clearing debris is not easy and, like success, must be intentional. If we cleave to what we've been through, it remains impossible for those around us to perceive our intentions. Because our intentions do not necessarily emerge through our actions, and instead are subverted by the many defense mechanisms that we've put in place to prevent the possibility of pain. To let go of the past takes great courage, to remove the debris takes great persistence, but if you believe as I do that the reward is worth the effort, then let the work begin.

How do we return as children and start anew? We find compelling wisdom from the prophet Ezekiel, whose words from God for the people of Israel resonate with similar power for us today. He wrote, "On the day you were born your cord was not cut, nor were you washed with water to make you clean, nor were you rubbed with salt or wrapped in cloths. No one looked on you with pity or had compassion enough to do any of these things for you. Rather, you were thrown out into the open field, for on the day you were born you were despised. Then I passed by and saw you kicking about in your blood, and as you lay there in your blood I said to you, 'Live!' " (Ezekiel 16:4–6, NIV).

This metaphoric description depicts the birth of a child who doesn't suffer from abuse or trauma but finds himself in a life-threatening circumstance merely by neglect. Often it's not what happened to us that shaped us but what did not happen to us that should have that shapes who we become. The cord was not cut, implying that we are still tied to where we started, unable to break free and live independently as our Creator intended. The debris of the birthing process was not removed, an essential cleansing in order for us to proceed to the next stage of life. And since the healing components were not added, we cannot experience a full recovery to health.

In spite of this gross negligence, God said one word, and this is "Live!" No one can go back and change the circumstances from which we were derived, but it's never too late to go back and cut your own cord, wash away the debris, obtain what you need for healing, and be free. All those around you will see the difference when they see your unencumbered self, your salted self, your washed-clean self, and notice that you are free from the aftereffects of past trauma.

Like a baby who no longer needs the umbilical cord, you are being challenged to cut away all the cords of the past abuse and neglect and thrust into your new life with the courage of children. Children speak honestly what they feel, forgive quickly, and run outside to play. They hug the same mommy who spanked them last night, play with the same friend who made fun of them yesterday, and imagine endless gardens growing through the cracks in their sidewalks. They always engage life with their most authentic selves. Wouldn't it be amazing if we could be children again?

It's not too late to claim your birthright! This is a great moment for you to rediscover who you were meant to be. Like a newborn emerging from the womb, we can find grace in each new day to be born again and again and again. And that's what makes people wonderful and exciting and interesting. This ability to change and grow and mature is what makes them a valuable asset to a company, makes them a great companion to another individual, makes them a compassionate parent to a child.

Every day is fascinating and holds endless potential because it's not contaminated with the encumbrances of yesterday. If we apply this principle of rebirth to our lives, then every man would find a new wife in the old one, every employer would find a new employee in the one she has, we would find a new self cut, cleaned, and salted because we would have a new heart, head, and mind.

No matter how old you are, you can be a child again. Those of us who have lived twenty-five years or longer know the urgency that intensifies within us as we long to change, to recapture the momentum of our early hopes, to glean the harvest from our field of dreams. It's too late to work out our dreams in a nursing home. We cannot pursue our full potential when we're incapacitated in assisted living. Eradicating the toxic infection of our wounded hearts is the most urgent need you have. It is time sensitive.

Reading this book may be the most important step you can take right now toward personal healing and professional advancement. It's not how you start but how you finish the race that counts. Before it's too late, let it go! It's time to get on with the real life you were meant to lead. It's time to *thrive*.

To embrace the life that awaits you, you must *let it go*!

one

Giants and Dwarfs

I have a confession to make and want you to hear it straight from me. It's about someone I love. *I am a lover of people who have big ideas!* I love the way they envision the world as an expansive landscape of ever-growing possibilities. What others see as insurmountable mountains or treacherous waters, they view as giant-sized opportunities and limitless horizons. I love to hear them talk because through them my own ideas are watered and fertilized by my exposure to their way of thinking. You see, I believe that one's speech is largely a result of his or her perspective. Generally, people's perspectives are born from the height in which they think.

Let me give you a very literal example. When my wife and I would hide our children's Christmas presents, I noticed an amusing propensity each of us had to hide the toys according to our respective heights. My wife hardly ever hid a present up high, keeping it within her arm's reach. Compared to me, she is relatively short in stature. So when she hid things, she always secured them in low places. I, conversely, hid the kids' toys in the top of the closet or in an air duct in the ceiling because my viewpoint reflected my height. My wife was not opposed to hiding them in high places; she simply didn't think to place them beyond her eye level. Her ideas were a reflection of her height.

For the past three hundred years, our country has largely been a big-idea nation. If you were to go back three centuries, a relatively short period in the history of the world, you would see that most of the modern conveniences we enjoy, like air travel, electricity, railroads, and automobiles, have only been in existence within the last one hundred years. Prior to the twentieth century, there were no computers, microwave ovens, no cell phones, car phones, or telephones at all. There were no engines, steam, gas, or electric motors. No indoor plumbing. No medical options like vaccinations, anesthesia, or chemotherapy. No major surgeries, such as heart replacements or kidney transplants. No stem cell research.

When one considers how long man has been in existence, the notion that most of the conveniences common to our present way of life only emerged in the past couple of centuries seems truly amazing. Their creation reveals that the last few generations have largely been the catalyst through which big ideas exploded and were massively produced.

Our country has thrived and become the envy of other nations because we have, for several generations, been a nation of big ideas. Big ideas come from forward-thinking people who challenge the norm, think outside the box, and invent the world they see inside rather than submitting to the limitations of current dilemmas.

Now, you might be scratching your head and saying, "What's he talking about? I thought this was a book about letting go of the past and finding the grace to forgive! Why is he going on and on about big ideas?" I am glad you asked. You see, much like turbo jets, fighter planes, the Internet, brain surgery, or stem cell research, forgiveness is a big idea. It takes a person who thinks big ideas rather than comparatively small thoughts to introduce and practice forgiveness effectively. Would you agree? Let's see if we can drill down into this notion to test its validity.

Releasing Revenge

Several years ago I was invited as a guest on *Oprah* to talk about sexual abuse. When I suggested that it is important that we move beyond just saying how bad the molester was to have committed such atrocious acts, to the larger (from my viewpoint) idea of showing the perpetrator how he can be forgiven and rehabilitated, people went wild. Some of the guests were far too angry to think beyond the height of the atrocities they had experienced. They used their anger like familiar blankets to warm them as a comfort from their trauma, never realizing how they were smothering their own futures. They couldn't imagine that future perpetrators will never come forward as long as they believe they have no chance at forgiveness and rehabilitation.

While the women who told their stories that day on the show had every justifiable reason to hate and be angry, the reality is that the poison of unquenched anger doesn't infect the perpetrator but only incarcerates the victim. Unforgiveness denies the victim the possibility of parole and leaves them stuck in the prison of what was, incarcerating them in their trauma and relinquishing the chance to escape beyond the pain.

We have seen this truth about forgiveness played out on a larger scale. When angry, bruised women from South Africa screamed in outrage because of the horrible atrocities they had been exposed to under apartheid, Nelson Mandela and members of the African National Congress (ANC) knew that a small idea like revenge would destroy the far larger idea of national healing and survival for their country. If they focused only on the temporary desire for immediate justice and swift retribution and missed the far weightier need for a healthy, functional, inclusive government in the midst of a nation filled with the pain of its most recent maladies, their homeland would never have survived.

The National Council of Provinces (NCOP) was developed to raise the bar by giving diplomatic immunity to sometimes undeserving people in order to protect the larger necessity of national survival. The big idea was forgiveness; the smaller idea, as justifiable as it might've been, was hatred, resentment, and revenge. South Africa survived because those at the helm chose the bigger idea of the good for all rather than the revenge of some.

When Dr. King resisted the lure of his own anger and submitted to the larger idea of a nonviolent movement that was led and filled with justifiably angry people, he preserved the future and changed our world. Those with the smaller ideas of starting our own country, or shooting and killing the racist molesters who had abused our fathers and raped our mothers, would have appeased our human need for retribution while destroying our way of life. We survived because we dared to risk acting on the larger notion of forgiveness rather than acquiesce to the dwarfed ideas of revenge and retaliation. Consequently, the destruction that would have been the inevitable result of thinking too small was eclipsed by the hopes of men and women who dared to dream on a scale larger than they had ever seen.

Like Native Americans relegated to a reservation where one could only be the chief of a small, government-sanctioned area, many of us remain on the reservation rather than escaping into the much larger world of assimilation, inclusion, and acceptance. Simply stated, people who don't forgive neutralize their own growth potential. They end up hopelessly entrapped by the repercussions of leadership that remains in a dwarfed context of thought, thereby missing the overarching need to transcend the immediate encumbrance. We must think beyond the reservation like so many Native Americans have done and move forward.

When I write on blogs and Facebook, I am often astonished at Christians who never leave the reservation and can only see or think from their own Christian perspective rather than evaluating others from a broader perspective of overall ability. They sacrifice an excellent leader because he isn't a Christian as they define it, or limit the discussion to one or two issues at the expense of the bigger idea of how well a leader can lead the country.

I shocked my church when I announced that I was far more interested in finding a surgeon who was great at operating than I was in finding one who voted like I did on political issues or shared my ideas on faith. I explained to them that I'm more concerned about a surgeon's track record in the arena of patient recovery success than I'm interested in interrogating him on his view of eschatological theology! I just want to know if he can do the job, not whether he teaches Sunday school at First Baptist!

On an operating table we can sacrifice the dwarfed idea of our personal theological perspectives for the bigger idea of a doctor's surgical competency. When we can have both, it's a real advantage. But I will not refuse the services of an excellent surgeon just because I don't like his favorite football team—or his religion!

Loosing Change

When looking at this model of thinking in our personal lives we must ask ourselves the question, Does incarcerating the perpetrator to a lifelong sentence with no hope of parole really protect us from the ever-increasing chances of attack by unknown stalk-ers? My fear is that it only perpetuates a pathology that teaches our children that we are too irrational a society to allow people to grow beyond what they did into what they can become. Con-sequently, perpetrators have no choice but to hide who they are and therefore continue to attack our children, destroy their mari-tal vows, or engage in disputes once mistakes are made. A healthy family environment is only achieved when one leaves the night-light on for those who have wandered away. We must be willing to give them what we all need, a GPS system that allows the prodigal son to find the way back when he is finally ready to return home.

I have learned that most people who harbor animosity in their hearts against others do so because they remain on the reserva-tion of what has happened in the past rather than escape to the much larger idea of a better future. However, they must ask them-selves, What will happen if I cling to my narrow perspective and lose a chance to loose change in my life? How can I move beyond my history into the larger terrain of my destiny?

Yes, ladies and gentlemen, forgiveness is a big idea and it works best when it is invested into people who have the courage to grasp the seven-foot-high idea of what's best for their future rather than the four-foot-high idea of recompense for what has happened in their past. I'm here to encourage you to cut the chain-link fence that prevents you from moving ahead by using the torch of big ideas to cut through the metal of a painful past. I suggest to you that forgiving the minor to protect the major is not only how civi-lizations survive, it's how individuals thrive!

You see, unforgiveness is a small sphere of operation. It exists among people who cannot escape what was for what is. The fam-ily that cannot forgive its members for poor past judgments will not easily survive. The child who is constantly assaulted by the relentless attacker castigating him for the foolish things he did yesterday will inevitably shrink, wither, and die, never becoming what he could have been had someone extended the nutrition of forgiveness. No, we must allow him to see that there is more to be considered before you than the total weight of all the mistakes left behind you.

This truth extends beyond the personal to the professional arena. With the exception of a few notable people who have continued to give us big ideas in the twenty-first century, today we mostly see tiny ideas camouflaged by slick, glossy advertising spin to try and hypnotize us into thinking this dwarf fits the stature of a big idea! Successful businesses must be constantly infused with big thinkers or they will quickly become obsolete and insolvent. If smaller businesses can't embrace change and adapt, then they will soon be taken over by bigger conglomerates that can move beyond the mom-and-pop stream into the ocean of higher-level thinking and consciousness.

Changing Clothes

Big ideas are only extracted from the hearts of big people who think beyond the breach and embrace the potential of the future. All of us are capable of big ideas and giant advancement, but we rarely experience the liberation of such large thinking. Unbeknownst to most of us, unforgiveness incarcerates us but never rehabilitates, and soon the warden of destruction becomes the coroner of death to our dreams, our hearts, and our hopes. When we do not embrace forgiveness as the key to our freedom, our little ideas will always poison our bigger opportunities for new thought, honest dialogue, and solution-oriented discussion.

The clarion call we get from God himself to forgive is a daunting challenge at best and will never be accomplished by those who will not forsake the comfort of anger for the challenge of moving ahead. As daunting as the talk may be, if we are to enjoy a brighter tomorrow, we must rid ourselves of the grave clothes of where we have been and stitch a newer garment of where we are going.

If you are a Christian reading this, you will likely remember that Jesus folded his death garments and appeared in the garden in bright apparel with no trace of where he had been lingering on him. Mary didn't even recognize Jesus, even though she knew him well, because he had moved to a new place of power, purpose, and peace. She was expecting him to look like and think like where he had been as opposed to where he was now!

Your past life is too small to fit you as you grow into the fullness of all you were meant to be. It's like wearing your sixth-grade band uniform to a symphony concert at Carnegie Hall! The garment is too small for where you are and where you are going, and to hold on to it is an expression of your constant need to see all things from the small perspective of a past experience.

Our nation and all nations who have enjoyed freedom did so only when they listened to a bigger idea than where they were at the time. If that is true for us as a civilization, it is also true of us as individuals. We are dwarfed down by the small pettiness of yesterday thinkers when what we really need can only come from those who think in an enlarged state of unleashed imagination!

Are you ready to change clothes? It is my hope as we embrace the challenges of higher-level thinking that we will inevitably, both as a society and more attainably as individuals, evolve beyond the dwarfed ideas that leave us captive to what was. It is my hope that those who think at an altitude beyond attitudes will find nourishment from this book to move far beyond pettiness into the powerful terrain of seven-foot-tall thinking. I believe that

God hides the answers to the questions we all want answered in higher places so that only eagles can find them and be nourished by them.

Flying High

The problem is that too many of us flounder as chickens rather than fly as eagles. While eagles soar and scan the skies, chickens are busy looking down and eating off the ground. Yes, they do survive from lower-level consumption, but they don't fly far or do much because they're too busy pecking at the ground below them. They never move beyond lower thinking into the power of spreading their wings like eagles and flying high.

Your mission—should you accept it—is to look up and consider who you are and where you're going. Will you choose to eat small-kernel thoughts off the ground, or will you seek the mountainous summits of success with those who overcome the giants of life and rise above the storm? As tasty as chicken may be to those who consume it, always remember that chickens mostly eat waste. Their overhead counterparts are too high to consume what was; eagles only eat what is.

Life is filled with giants and chickens live in fear of them. Especially with their heads looking down, they could be squashed, decapitated, or destroyed. Their vulnerability is that they remain within the reach of the giants of possible destruction. Giants only fight what they can reach. They only find the treasure that lies in low places. So chickens and those who have chicken ideas are always in the reach of those who seek to destroy them.

In my other business of entertainment, chickenlike movies don't often achieve box office acclaim. More times than not, little investment means little return. Hollywood producers invest the biggest monies into what they believe to be the bigger ideas. The giants of low expectations cause them to underfund chicken entertainment, eat up those drumstick profits, and move on. Though I understand this paradigm, and even have operated on a chicken business level, more times out of necessity than preference, I hold in my heart eagle ideas waiting to be unveiled.

If you have lived with chickens but thought like an eagle, it is only a matter of time before someone will see the eagle in you and allow you to spread your wings and fly higher. But keep in mind, if you want to go for it as an eagle, you must let go of the chicken's perspective. Don't let the giant problems, budget restrictions, or even legitimate excuses deter your dreams and overpower your passions.

You may start on the ground, but for God's sake end up in the air! From the eagle's view, the giants shrink and become inconsequential. From the eagle's view, new opportunities are always within sight. The eagle sees what lies before him while the chicken's view is only what lies beneath him! Eagles never fear giants because they dwell too high to live at risk!

Don't get me wrong—I love chickens and have taken care of them, fed them, and even eaten them. But I don't write to them! For the closet eagles reading this material, it's time to spread your wings and lift your vision. We are about to sail far beyond our yesterdays into the cerulean celestials of what lies before us. If forgiveness is a big idea—and it is—then you will need a full set of long wings to rise above the temporal and sail into the transcendent. It's time to consider what you could attain if you cast off the weight of yesterday and embrace the galling winds of a changed mind and an open heart.

Cancer of the Soul

My fear is that if we don't learn to fly as the eagles soar, then we unwittingly set ourselves up to become the burial ground for land mines. Or to use a more powerful, even shocking metaphor, unforgiveness unchecked becomes a cancer in our soul. Just like the fear we all have of discovering a malignancy within our own body, we must learn to be vigilant regarding the grudges we harbor and the offenses we experience. Otherwise, we may never see it coming.

We all fear the nightmare of cancer, and you cannot be alive today and not be touched by it, either directly or within your family or by someone you love. It's the moment when our worst nightmare is unleashed, when a routine physical becomes a terminal diagnosis, or when a small nagging ache belies a much greater problem within. A tumor is discovered or cancer cells are spotted, a polyp or lump emerges from hiding.

Far too many people go in for a checkup and are shocked to find that they are in the fourth stage of cancer. Never saw it coming, no warning signs, and no symptoms, just slammed to the floor. It is difficult for them and painful for the family. Seemingly there was no preparation time; it just came out of nowhere.

Looking back, it may now seem that carefree days spent basking in the luxurious warmth of the sun became the entry point for the malignant growth of melanoma. While many cancers may not be avoidable, there are some healthy habits that could help many of us live our lives without having to deal with what some call "the battle of a lifetime." Either through ignorance and lack of education (we certainly never used sunscreen when I was growing up!), or through the recklessness or carelessness of youth (when we can't imagine wrinkles and sunspots, let alone shielding our skin to prevent something as ominous as cancer), we failed to do all that we could to ensure our body's health. And now we're paying the price through a debilitating battle with a cancer that threatens to diminish our quality of life permanently.

Early Detection

I have noticed whenever my wife is scheduled to have a mammogram, her voice will often convey the hidden anxiety she harbors about what such a test might reveal. She will tell me she is about to take that test and there is always a slight quiver in her voice. She has never had cancer, but living with the potential and having witnessed what many friends have gone through gives her some trepidation when she goes in for testing. There is always the potential that some invasion has occurred unbeknownst to her, that she could have cancer and not know it. The older I get, the more I feel the same sense of anxious uncertainty whenever I go in for a checkup or routine medical procedure.

While I certainly advocate doing everything humanly possible to prevent cancer and promote early detection, my purpose here is not to alarm you about this disease but to make you aware of its emotional and spiritual equivalent that is just as detrimental and life altering. Our inability or unwillingness to forgive past offenses often festers and metastasizes within us, quietly growing into a blockage that impedes every area of our lives. Unforgiveness can silently lurk in our own hearts as well as the hearts of people we love and remain undetected until it dramatically reveals itself in a crisis or emotional breakdown.

When the malignancy of a past wound is revealed, everyone involved feels shocked because they never dreamed that such pain, rage, vitriol, and animosity could exist beneath the surface of this person who continued to make breakfast, celebrate holidays, and buy them roses. If you have lived long enough, you know that it's virtually impossible to really know all about someone, to see into their hearts and know what's going on below the surface. Emotional wounds do not always have outward signs of inward turmoil.

Most people fail to perform emotional self-examinations, and too often if they do, they ruminate on what they find instead of seeking resolution and healing. Similarly, we fail to conduct routine checks to ensure that the persons we work with or live with are really being open and honest with their feelings. I fear that the busyness of our lives lends itself to assumptions, expectations, and considerations that often allow unresolved issues from our past to multiply into a cancerous growth within our soul. Ignoring the accumulation of wounds, offenses, slights, and injustices that we have endured can lead to an outbreak of serious problems that debilitate relationships and end productivity.

Much like the removal of moles and skin lesions is done to prevent them from growing into more serious skin abnormalities, removing minor discord before it becomes a calamity is an important use of our time. Most people don't like to make waves and they swallow frustration and bury true feelings, not wanting to compromise temporary tranquility, never realizing that massive turmoil doesn't start out massive—it grows beneath the skin like a cancer that could have been avoided with early detection. My friend, people resign from a job long before they type the letter. Husbands leave before they move out. Children rebel in their hearts before getting arrested for vandalism.

We take for granted that if we don't feel anything or see anything, then everything must be okay. But some of the most lethal killers of our natural health are the silent ones. High blood pressure doesn't make a sound. Cancer can eat inwardly for months and produce not one symptom outwardly to warn you it has taken root inside the body. This is why everyone should have checkups and regular medical exams. Similarly, this is why we must perform checkups on our emotional and attitudinal health as well as those around us. I don't mean navel-gazing about why someone hurt your feelings at the church picnic or tossing out a drive-by statement like "how are you doing?" We have to set aside time to really communicate what's going on inside us and discover what's really going on inside the other person if we want to foster an atmosphere of health, well-being, and intimacy.

Yes, too often we never see it coming. Just as the cancer patient thought of herself as a healthy person prior to the dreaded discovery and diagnosis, we often assume that we are okay as long as we keep up the hectic pace of everyday life. When warning signs emerge in our relationships, our business deals, and our personal friendships, we ignore them or dismiss them as insignificant and unworthy of a more thorough examination.

Often people so honor or respect us that they smother discontentment to appear congenial. This kind of deception is often well-meaning but can really rob us of a fighting chance at a better atmosphere at home and at work. Just because a person shows up at work and completes basic assignments doesn't ensure that they are really fulfilled in the workplace. Just because our kids give us a sweet card on Mother's Day doesn't mean that our relationship rivals those on the *Cosby Show*! Just because our spouse sits across from us at dinner and smiles doesn't mean that our hearts are in sync together.

I have seen, time and time again, frustration imitate cancer and silently engulf people who avoid confrontation to the point of becoming martyrs simply because they lack the courage or the skills to be forthcoming about little areas of discontentment and resentment. Before you know it, you have lost a very good staff person to the silent progression of a discontentment that could have been avoided by communicating small things before they became major. Or consider the wife who never realized how restless and dissatisfied her husband had grown in their marriage until an affair was revealed. Many friendships and relationships are often stuck on a treadmill of superficial niceness because neither person is willing to examine their grievances and express their concerns. Forgiveness, as we will explore, requires daily practice rather than the pressure of crisis management.

The Art of Forgiveness

The other insidious danger of not practicing forgiveness is that we become contagious carriers of the very offenses that we ourselves have suffered. If we saw our parents use violence to handle conflict, then that's how we assume we should handle conflict. If we were betrayed by an untrustworthy partner, then we're tempted to resort to the same tactics to avoid being betrayed again ourselves. Or consider this: Researchers discovered decades ago that the vast majority of child molesters were themselves sexually abused as children.

Now, that's not to say that everyone who suffered abuse as a child is destined to become an abuser. Some face eating disorders, promiscuity, or other scars like low self-esteem. Not only people suffering with these issues, but also all of us who have had some deeply painful moments of life. Not all rise to that level but inevitably not one of us will live and die without our tear ducts being used along the way. The goal is to protect our future from being infected with the many woes of our past. This is no easy flip-an-emotional-switch kind of process, I realize. So if you are thinking,

"If you knew what I've been through in my life, then you would understand why I could never forgive the people who hurt me," please know that I understand the enormous difficulty of your burden.

However, I also know that God did not design us to be victims. Even as we experience the selfish, painful, sometimes evil choices of other people, we are not without the same power to choose not to be further molested by the ghost of our hideous experiences. We always have a choice. The tragedy is that so many people become trapped in hell long after their wounds were inflicted. Just as our bodies are designed to heal and recover from our physical injuries, our souls want to help us to recover from the internal wounds that we've suffered. Without realizing it, however, we are often the ones holding up the process because we do not have the tools, the role models, the maturity, or the spiritual insight to move forward and allow healing to take place. We have not learned early-detection procedures that would allow us to enjoy a healthier, more balanced quality of life.

My hope is that this book will provide you with all of these most vital elements in practicing the art of forgiveness. And please understand that in order to forgive others, we must be willing to look at our own ability to hurt, offend, and injure those around us, often the people we love the most. As we will discover, the Lord's Prayer provides us with a key insight into how we can experience the joy and abundant life that Jesus told us he came to bring. "Give us this day our daily bread, and forgive us our trespasses as we forgive those who trespass against us," Jesus taught us to pray (Matthew 6:11–12, KJV).

I fear that many people do not realize when they pray this most famous prayer that they are asking God to forgive them in the same way that they themselves are forgiving (or not forgiving) other people! I do not believe God is punishing us in this manner, telling us that basically we'll receive from him the same thing we've been dishing out to others. God is much bigger than that, much more loving, gracious, and compassionate to us his children. No, what I believe Jesus reveals in the Lord's Prayer is that our human capacity to receive God's grace is blocked when we are not willing to forgive those who have hurt us. We cannot embrace God's forgiveness if we are so busy clinging to past wounds and nursing old grudges. In order to move into the blessings of our future, we must relinquish the pains of the past.

Forgiveness doesn't exonerate the one who hurt you nor does it trivialize the depth of your trauma. No, not at all. What it does do is liberate you and your soul from living in the Amityville Horror house of memories and agonies that aren't worthy of more time in your life. Forgiveness, then, is a gift you must find a way to give yourself regardless of who or what has dropped you into this grievous state of affairs. I earnestly believe that unforgiveness is the leading cause of divorce—not adultery or even economics, which are often touted as the culprits. It has been a sword devastating sisters, mothers, fathers, and countless sons. It has damaged office relationships and undermined the teamwork that increases profit margins and coalesces the best of the best into a business model with higher yields and greater proficiency!

So, then, forgiveness is essential if we are to grow into the fullness of who God created us to be. As we are made in his image, we share his capacity to love, to experience betrayal from those we love, and to extend forgiveness and risk loving again. Forgiveness isn't about weakening you but strengthening you to live again and love again, performing at your highest capacity, unencumbered by yesterday's maladies. I want to coach you back to your fullest potential and stop the brain drain and agony of a memory gone wild. And help you regain your control as you do have enormous power to change the quality and direction of your own life, away from the path of soul stagnation and bitterness and toward the spiritual healing of grace and peacefulness.

Do you really want to experience the fullness of the life you were meant to lead, a life of contented purpose, creative vitality, and joyful intimacy with those you love? Are you willing to let go of the chronic emotional ache from the many blows you've experienced in life? Can you sense that now is your season of transition from the old, cracked, and chipped containers of your energy to the joy of new wineskins?

Then it's time to experience the supernatural power that's unleashed when we *let it go*!

two
Offenses Do Come

Though I am a Christian, I understand that many of the world's major religions share spiritual truths that transcend time and culture and reflect a universal understanding of human nature and the seasons of one's life. Whether you call it karma, fate, destiny, or the Golden Rule, I believe that one of these truths can be summed up by the adage that you reap what you sow. In the course of life, the offended and the offender will both change places from time to time. People who trespass on the emotional property of others' lives will someday find their own property invaded.

Even if the offender never suffers at the hands of the same people they've offended, life ensures that what goes around will eventually come back around. The one who constantly injures others, leaving a trail of collateral damage in their wake like a human Hurricane Katrina, will eventually find themselves caught in someone else's emotional tsunami. The cheater will be cheated on; the thief will be stolen from. As the old song says, the hunter will occasionally get captured by the game!

Even the most even-tempered, mild-mannered, self-effacing individuals will at some time or another rock someone else's boat. Even the most ruthless, raucous, rambunctious risk-taker will find themselves seasick from the waves caused by someone else's risk. No matter how you acquiesce to others and try to be subservient and kind, eventually you will have to stand for something, and when you do, someone is going to be offended. No matter how bold, aggressive, and proactive you are in protecting yourself from life's blows, someone will still manage to discover your vulnerability and hurt you. It is impossible to live this life without some conflict along the way. The wise planner thinks in terms of this inevitability and develops a strategy that doesn't leave you devastated when they do.

Certainly if you knew you and your friend would one day be at odds, maybe you wouldn't have confided in him so deeply. If you'd known that your daughter wouldn't repay the loan, you might have reconsidered cosigning. Who would've foreseen that your marriage would end with you screaming obscenities at someone you once caressed and to whom whispered sweet nothings?

We all start with optimism or we wouldn't begin the initiative. In business most deals start positively. A dinner meeting is scheduled and enjoyed, cocktails at five or a discussion over nine holes of golf. Projections are shown, pitches are made, and deals are done. In marriage most couples are happy at the wedding and some even make it through the honeymoon, but life isn't comprised of white lace and promises, romantic vacations to deserted islands. Running a company will eventually mean navigating the rough terrain of terminating people, budget cuts, and upsetting the initial tranquility. Every marriage will be strained by the storms of life and the trials of loving and living with someone who does not see things exactly the way you do.

Wise people plan in advance the terms of resolution while hoping they will never need to use them. Some contracts include an arbitration clause to set up rules when business has gone awry and someone is offended. In marriage many couples participate in premarital counseling in order to anticipate where they will experience conflicts and how they will resolve them. Many also include a prenup just in case they don't make it to the happily-ever-after part of life! Unfortunately, most of us have learned the hard way how to face conflict and handle disappointment. Most of us were never taught to understand human psychology and motivation or equipped with tools of arbitration and negotiation. Depending on the basis for our expectations, we may have been in for quite a surprise!

Unarmed and Dangerous

Now, I date myself by sharing this, but I was raised when family television programs seldom had meaningful offenses or realistic conflicts. From Fat Albert cartoons to *The Brady Bunch,* we watched seemingly flawless characters navigate their near-perfect lives through simplistic problems that were generally resolved by the end of the episode, usually in a predictable, humorous manner with a clichéd life lesson learned.

Perhaps subconsciously, I, like many others, expected to embark on a life filled with temporary problems that could be fixed quickly. Equipped with simple solutions and examples of harmonious relationships I'd witnessed on television, I expected my life to reflect the domestic tranquility of Aunt Bee's front porch swing.

Little did I know that life does not reflect a scripted entertainment segment but is instead often filled with complex issues, conflicted people, and complicated situations that cannot be easily resolved before the next commercial break. Somehow these seemingly benign sitcoms fueled my imagination like cheap gas in a Toyota, filling me with a philosophical ideology based on punch lines and laugh tracks, miles away from the unexpected dramas that awaited me in real life. Expecting a scenic drive through Mayberry, I was unprepared for the off-road excursion that would require me to blaze my own trail through the wilderness of unmarked territory.

As I traveled deeper into my journey, I learned that it is often the lofty expectations that give us the most pain. It is the misguided notions often induced by what we saw on television or read in a book that make us want life to pattern art rather than the other way around. Instead of the naïve indulgence of perfect people who have warm and affirming experiences and live out their perfect little lives, I would learn how to steer through the maze of relationships, issues, and conflicts inherent within the human condition.

If the truth were told, neither school nor church prepares us to manage our disappointment when our basic human needs and expectations aren't met. Most parents, teachers, and clergy are themselves ill-equipped to manage the many times and various ways that life can pierce us to the core and leave us gasping in pain, shocked that those closest to us could become the catalyst for so much anguish and dis-ease. We go out unarmed for the assaults of life and become overwhelmed by the emotional danger we encounter.

What to Expect When You're Expecting

No matter where we are in our lives, we all continue to have hopes, aspirations, and expectations. But if we haven't stopped to question what we've learned and consider how it's working for us, then we set ourselves up for repeated failure. Our expectations have a direct effect on the level of our disappointment and our perception of the offenses we receive. Usually, we think we can and should expect more from those we love than what they often deliver.

And it doesn't end with our private relationships but often infiltrates the places where we work and worship. Most people carry their longing for blissful idealism with them when they go into the public square. Their need to love and be loved leaks into their professional life and sets them up for the same disappointing response as they attempt to develop a private level of intimacy in a public arena. The real culprit dwells in their expectations.

Some people bring great grief on themselves because they are unable to differentiate the necessary boundaries and reasonable expectations between their professional and personal lives. Understanding the difference between what you can expect from a professional relationship and a private one would have saved many people their job. As I often say, this is not that!

When you handle your coworkers like they are personal friends you open yourself up for the possibility of offense. Just because you share an office doesn't mean you have to share secrets. It is one thing to have an amiable working relationship and it is quite another for me to share my life with you. Just because you work in the same building or we share the same cubicle, I am not required to relinquish my personal boundaries.

You can be gracious and helpful without expecting the person who relates to you on the job to be like your cousins who come over for a fish fry! How many times do I see people get personal with those whom they should have kept at a respectful and cordial distance? In most cases, their disappointment comes from the lack of delineation between the two types of relationship!

Or conversely they are forever trying to bring their friends into a business deal. Sometimes it is harmful to do business with friends and relatives. Not everyone has the ability to function with you on multiple levels without losing what you had to begin with. Next thing you know, you have created a wedge between where you started and where you are trying to go. Friends-turned-business partners often wind up feeling betrayed or disappointed because someone said something or violated a trust that you should have never placed in them in the beginning.

In reality it is important to realize that, like rain, offenses will come, often unexpectedly. No matter how wonderful the initial experiences are, how optimistically the first day at work may have gone, how special the child is that is born to the best possible parents, the disappointments will come. The child will at some time disappoint the parents and the parents eventually will disappoint the child. The first day at work will eventually lead to a bad day at work.

Offenses come to everyone. From the articulate intellectual to the most formidable illiterate, from the most conservative political perspective to the most liberal worldview, the one common denominator among all social classes is that you cannot exist in this world without encountering various types of offenses and disappointments. The difference in people emerges in how they respond to the conflicts they encounter.

Broken Handles

Since these offenses are as organic to life as the need for water, the distinction between people is indeed how we handle those conflicts. Top-level executives are employed based on their ability to manage those conflicts and to mitigate the possible damages and liabilities associated with their organization. In effect, each of us has a responsibility to see the bigger picture or purpose and avoid the propensity to blind ourselves by micromanaging and staring at minute issues until they resemble mountains.

If we allow our reactions to reflect our pettiness and short-sightedness, then we miss the larger opportunity to move forward and effectively grow into new and greater responsibilities. Too often we become ensnared by the traffic jam of conflicts and disappointment and find ourselves trying to drive forward while our eyes are affixed to the rearview mirror.

I have come to learn that when we say to ourselves, to our God, or to anyone that we can't handle the conflict, we are in essence saying we can't handle the promotions of life. For every promotion brings each of us into a higher level of exposure to conflict. If you can't handle the pressure, you can't function in the promise that is inherent to that level of promotion. If you don't want to work through marital problems, don't get married. If you don't want to have to rush down to the parent-teacher meeting, don't have children. If you don't want a flat tire, don't drive a car.

Some people recognize that problems and flat tires occur but erroneously assume that they only happen to other people. They work hard to convince themselves that they are the exception to the realities of life and human nature. "My husband would never disrespect or humiliate me," they say. "My daughter would never betray my trust," they insist. "My business associate would never leave to work for a competitor," they maintain. But in reality the best of us often disappoint even those we love the most, let alone those we work with or for every day. We fail to realize that what offends one person is a joke to another. Part of the hurt is a result of the expectation that offenses aren't a part of every relationship. And what makes some survive and others fail is how they manage those offenses when they do occur.

People Phobia

In the absence of such strategies, we often retract into our shell, a logical reaction but one that is nonetheless detrimental to our career, our marriage, and our self worth. Often the most embittered, callous people are actually the most sensitive. From my experiences, I have come to realize that often the most creative, giving, sincere people have the greatest likelihood to carry the cancer of unforgiveness.

They do so in part because they enter into each arena of life expecting more than they receive and have no template to manage the disappointments of life. They assume because they are sincere and well intentioned that all others are, too. I am becoming increasingly aware that people persons often carry the most pain and unforgiveness because they are the most likely to expect so much more than is feasible from those least likely to deliver.

They embrace an idea that suggests that everyone else is having a wonderful life and somehow they can't seem to get it right! It is the feeling that the offense is abnormal and unusual and hence they feel guilty that they are having trouble and also feel cheated that they are seemingly the only one dealing with such tragic circumstances. They have judged themselves a failure because they do not realize that offenses are common and a part of the relationship.

This juvenile need for victory without conflict, pleasure without any pain, can leave you the most wounded because this child-like naïveté makes us more likely to suffer injury to the soul and bury it in silence. Like those who have delicate skin, they are more apt to be bruised or sunburned; those who are the most creative or sensitive feel the most violated by the behavior of others. The very thing that makes them an asset can also make them a liability: sensitivity! Because they care the most, they often carry the deepest scars from the painful disappointments, eventually squashing their creativity and leaving them disenfranchised with work systems, personal investment, and creative input. They simply become so guarded that all that could've been accomplished suffers in the silence.

The disappointments with life in general, coupled with a simmering inferno over the details of what they've suffered, typically produce bitter, unforgiving people. Bitterness can leave you as disfigured inwardly as a bad face-lift can leave you distorted outwardly. And if you have ever seen a face-lift gone badly, you understand what I mean!

Once we incur such a debilitating wound, we usually develop the yellow-brick-road complex. Like Dorothy in *The Wizard of Oz*, we see any new date, new acquaintance, or new team member as "lions, tigers, and bears" waiting to pounce on us and inflict more injury. Consequently, we approach new situations with a deep and sometimes painful skepticism. When you operate from a position of victimization, you come into the future with the toxic waste from the past.

Every comment made at a dinner party is later dissected and overanalyzed. We see goblins in the shadows of every new encounter and without knowing it we develop a people phobia. We then self-sabotage our success with the sniper fire of overscrutinizing every encounter. If any of these descriptions sound remotely like you, then hang on because help is on the way!

Unwrapped Presents

Wherever you find people, you will find lurking within them the potential to incur offenses. For some who are more anal and less social, this is all the excuse they need for a complete retreat to the land of "I don't care," though they really do! But this reclusiveness provides less potential for damage. They like to play it safe. They do not seek socialization but rather trust in the reliability of hard drives, equipment, paintbrushes, pet care, or anything that relieves them of the need to engage people on a level for which they may risk damage. They simply live in a perpetual state of avoidance.

The problem with this approach is that your prosperity and personal well-being require you to have good people skills (or are at least enhanced when you do)! This fear of people and intimacy can distort our true nature, leaving kind, gregarious people spectators rather than participators in life, hiding our true inner selves, unwilling to risk further damage to the soul. They spend their lives like unwrapped gifts beneath the proverbial Christmas tree: never giving what they have for fear of losing what they've got. Remember, you can't give it away and save it at the same time.

Because you were born to love and born to give, not doing so can affect every area of your life. Your work suffers because the true power of your gift is submerged beneath your fear of betrayal, and with its drowning comes the loss of a healthy work environment and more times than not limits on income opportunities, promotions, and advancement.

To cut to the bottom line, unforgiveness is expensive! It can cost you money! This self-indulgence in pain is expensive. People in the workplace allow you to fail, as you don't build relationships well. It causes you to miss opportunities because people don't get to see what you can do. You are buried beneath the weight of resentment.

Success doesn't materialize for you simply because the asset that you could be to a company, a spouse, a child, or an organization is buried beneath the person you think you have had to become to protect who you could have been from what happened to you before!

And because your commitment to the issue of offense is stronger than your commitment to moving ahead, the prosperity in your public and private lives pays a huge toll. New relationships grind and sputter, new business deals hiss and jerk, suffering like a car being driven with the emergency brake still engaged. It isn't that you don't move forward, but the grinding of your reservations thwarts the creativity and vibrancy you were created to give.

Living this way suffocates the vibrancy of your life, leaving a mere shadow of who you would've been if you weren't driving with the brake grinding in your heart. The real danger lies in the need to be emotionally and creatively safe driving every decision and thereby taking precedence over the major contribution you could be to those you love, those you work with, and those to whom you have been exposed.

Opportunities in Disguise

I have learned what I'm sharing here the hard way. As I mentioned, I have had to let go of my TV-based set of expectations and reeducate myself in the classroom of life experiences. One situation in particular comes to mind in which one of my most frustrating experiences blossomed into one of my most compelling opportunities. You may find the life lesson I learned quite surprising.

Many years ago, I was asked to speak for a very large, prestigious faith-based organization. Thrilled beyond what I could've ever imagined in my little community in the hills of West Virginia, I was awestruck at such a great opportunity to speak to thousands of people and immediately accepted this amazing invitation. My host described the conference and advised me to bring products like tapes from previous sermons. Having only one tape duplicator, which produced three tapes at a time, I appreciated having advance notice to prepare and produce enough tapes for this gathering of thousands.

This opportunity was not only exciting for me but for my church as well. We were a small church and saw this situation as part of God's provision for us. We were hoping to raise enough from the product sales of this engagement to help us get in the building we were trying to purchase. We were all pitching in, having bake sales, and anything else we could do to buy supplies so we could prepare materials, hoping that they would sell well and help us move closer to our dream of having a real church building and not just the rundown facility we had partially converted.

A few weeks before the event, we got a letter saying that we would be required to sell all of our products through their bookstore with a whopping 25 percent off-the-top consignment fee. By the time I calculated the overhead, shipping, and unit cost, I found our return on the product investment was down to nothing if we had to pay the 25 percent tax they required. The alternative—tacking the 25 percent onto the price paid by the customer—meant the risk of losing the sale completely. The small honorarium they were paying me was nowhere near the 25 percent we would be losing. We were in a real fix!

Being the kind of person who will speak up, especially about unfair business practices, I asked about this requirement. In response, I was told by the host ministry that this fee was out of their control; it was a result of the venue where this massive event was to be held and consequently could not be changed. I accepted this explanation at face value since I was totally out of my element and had never participated in such a large event. In other words, I didn't know then what I do now! I've since learned that most rented venues require some kickback on concessions, which is often negotiated out of the deal in advance of the event. Most venues will take a flat fee if negotiations occur before the contract is signed and the fee paid. But maybe they didn't know enough to do that and perhaps were caught as I was between a rock and a hard place.

I tried not to allow my disappointment to color my preparation and focus, and I remained so excited and grateful for the opportunity. I spoke that night, the response was phenomenal, and the public bought everything we had! I was so excited to be received so well. And I thought no more about the product consignment fee as I was more focused on the warm reception that accompanied my debut at this new level.

Little did I realize that some of the poison of my resentment lingered in my bloodstream. Months later I was invited back for the same organization, only this time they rented a church instead of a public arena and wanted me to again serve as the keynote speaker. I felt sure that they had rented a supersized church to avoid whatever contractual problem they were trying to explain to me the previous time.

Once again my deacons, friends, and relatives met in our church in Charleston, cranked up the tape duplicator, and began production on more material to sell at this next event. Since we had sold out at the previous event, we even borrowed several tape duplicators from an old friend of mine so that we could keep up with demand. We were all so grateful and said, "Wow! This is the

Lord helping us get our own building. How wonderful is that?" Unbeknownst to us, however, was the fact that we were once again working with a very different set of expectations than our host organization operated from.

You can guess what happened. A week out from the blessed event, I got the same letter about products being taxed 25 percent. This time I was livid—I thought my blood pressure was going to come boiling out the top of my head like a volcano! It was suddenly quite clear that this pastor was charging us concessions just like a secular building might. It was clear to me that they were exploiting me and taking advantage of the situation. And they knew there was nothing I could do about it. Feeling like an abused child, I had to smile in front of everyone or risk losing the chance of a lifetime to minister from their large platform.

Fight for Flight

By the time of the second event, I was seething inside. Once again, I preached to the best of my ability, the response was overwhelming, and all of my materials sold out. And as the evening winded down, I couldn't hold it inside any longer. I couldn't wait to square off with the business administrator or whoever was in charge and just have it out! While I am not usually argumentative, I am terribly protective of those I love. And this felt like a blatant slap in the face of my members who had worked so hard for the goal we all shared. If we were going to be exploited, then I was at least going to put up a good fight. Needless to say, the teddy bear in me had turned grizzly!

A few minutes later, I found myself behind the church in a very heated argument with the business officer from the organization. I told him, "I bought the line about a mandatory fee on concessions on the last deal, but now that we're here at a church with no union and no contracts for concessions, why would you allow greed to exploit your guest like this?" The place had been packed to the rafters both times with over ten thousand people in attendance. I was sure the people had been generous enough in the offerings to underwrite the budget. Why would this huge organization with so much going for itself take away our little congregation's hope of having a church we could call our own? In essence I felt that they were prostituting my gift.

The gentleman began stumbling and stuttering, clearly shocked that someone who had just finished preaching could turn around and sound like a Philadelphia lawyer putting him on trial! He was clearly caught off guard and could not give me a clear answer. It was evident that he felt sympathetic to my plight and was just reciting the instructions he'd been given. I said, "Don't tell me that the host church is charging you all a service fee on concessions, because if you do, I am going to go ask their pastor!"

Based on his response, I was absolutely positive they were running a scam on me and I became even more incensed and outraged. I thought of all the nights my little church and I had been up till daybreak preparing our cassettes and covers, singing and praying as we worked for this mammoth opportunity. I thought of how I had told the bank that when I returned, we would have the money needed to close the deal.

The more I thought about our church mothers on their knees stuffing the tape cases and praying for God to bless us, the angrier I became. But then something happened that changed the tenor of the conversation and ultimately changed my life. Right in the middle of my tirade, the gentleman said tearfully, "I don't want to argue with you. I was so blessed by your message that I felt like God spoke something to me that I must obey." I was taken aback at the sincerity in his voice. He continued, "I want to serve your ministry and vision. I feel called to help you. I feel like God wants me to help you get on television." Talk about stopping me in my tracks!

For a moment, I thought he was patronizing me in the worst way possible. I thought, "Television? I'm not about to get on television!" We had almost no money in the bank at all. We only had two hundred members, and we didn't see a hundred of them until holidays like Easter and Christmas Eve!

How in the world would I get on TV? The more I thought about what this man was saying, the crazier it seemed. I didn't have a deal with a network, I didn't own a television camera, or have any significant staff. If I were to get the opportunity to go on national TV, I didn't even have access to a studio or any facility for shooting. Little did I know that in that moment, God was birthing an opportunity out of my offense. Like Joseph confronting his brothers in Egypt, I realized that what others may have intended for their own greed was now being transformed by God into Joseph's good.

I was still seething so it took a minute for his humbled words to make it through the fog of my fury. But my intellect told my emotions to shut up and be quiet. My inner spirit bore witness that this was to be a God moment in my life.

Over time and through prayer, I received one of the greatest opportunities of my ministry, one that would alter the course of my life and history. It changed my life forever, and without it I wouldn't even have reached whatever accomplishments I have had. The only reason I share it with you now is to present evidence that sometimes the greatest opportunities are hidden in the deepest moments of offense. If you aren't strong enough to check your emotions, you can miss a great opportunity or misjudge a wonderful person caught in a bad situation. That guy who was combative at the time became one of my greatest allies and helped me accomplish so much in my life.

I am so thankful that he and I didn't define each other by one or two incidents. If nothing else, offenses can be chances for character development and a true thermometer for maturity development. Thank God I didn't let the spirit of offense make me miss a moment that had been ordained to bless me. I had to get over the smaller issue to see the larger plan of what God was doing in my life. I had seen him work through good times, but now I was seeing him use adversity for advancement!

Right or Rewarded

Even now, armed with thirty-five years of heading a very large faith-based organization, I still look back and think to myself, I was right in my assertion I was being used. I have traveled all over the world and have never encountered such a deal again. I was correct that the 25 percent taxation on sale merchandise we brought with us was so unfair that it should have provoked the Boston Tea Party! But that isn't the important thing to remember. Just because the facts are on your side doesn't mean you know the truth that matters. Would you rather be right or be rewarded?

The important thing to remember is that my greatest opportunity was born in the middle of an offense. I learned that day that it is possible to be right about the issue but you can be wrong to take on the fight. Sometimes you have to learn that offense is the midwife of opportunity!

Had I not listened to my inner voice I would have missed a

great opportunity to speak to millions of people that night because I was angry over what had happened with thousands. I had
to learn to see the bigger picture!

Today I have no anger for the organization, the church involved, or anyone else, as I know that offenses do come. I realize
that I was young, uncertain, intimidated, and perhaps a bit sensitive. If you accept the terms you live with them. If you don't accept
them, don't go. I could have canceled the products and just spoke.
I could have not spoken at all, but I couldn't change the rules in
another man's house just because I had a need. They had no obligation to treat me any particular way. I needed the faith to trust
God when the way he takes you looks like a wilderness and seems
unfair.

You can be blessed with new opportunities and be blindsided
by an inability to control something that you have just been introduced to yourself. Be still and wait. It is through incidents like this
that the acrid dis-ease of bitterness can set up the first cells that
lead to the ultimate cancerous conditions in our souls.

If you allow offense to have free rein, it will eat up opportunities you didn't even know were waiting just beyond the test! All
of us want the blessing, but we don't always have the life skills to
manage the stress that goes along with stewarding and maintaining that blessing. Who would think that you can have a car that
never needs repair? Or a house with no maintenance? Similarly,
any life worth living faces conflict with a variety of tools from
which wisdom can be gleaned, a relationship improved, or an opportunity revealed.

When Jesus said that "offenses do come," he offered us a
warning that offenses are an inevitable part of all relationships.
Yet most people have no provision in their thought process that

includes a healthy plan to function when the relationship, agreement, ally, or staff person has become dysfunctional, disloyal, or diseased. Don't wait till it rains to buy an umbrella! Now is the time to become informed and equipped so that you can repair the damage of past storms and confidently face the conflicts of the future.

three
Where Did This Come From?

_____

As we have discussed, offenses do indeed come for all of us. No human being wants to suffer the disappointment, hurt, betrayal, or loss that comes when someone injures us, either intentionally or unknowingly. Yes, offenses may appear out of thin air, arriving in our lives without warning, inflicted by people we thought we could trust. But the question that looms largest at the heart of forgiveness is how we respond to the offense.

Many people often experience the same or similar tragedies, but rarely do we respond the same way. Some people become bitter and defensive and step into a suit of armor at the smallest offense. Someone they barely know doesn't fawn over them, and suddenly these people act like Saint Peter has passed them by at the pearly gates! Others inspire us with their graciousness, mercy, and compassion by quickly forgiving the most heinous crimes against them. While they may reasonably be outraged and cut to the quick at the core of their being, these individuals display maturity, faith, and hope.

You see, the same heat that hardens the clay melts the wax. Since we cannot control when offenses will come or through whom they will arrive, then we can only control the way in which we experience them. At the core of forgiveness is an acute self-awareness about how we monitor and manage our reactionary thoughts, feelings, and behavior.

Default Settings

One of the primary ways we can begin to take control of the forgiveness process is to examine our personal default settings. If you are like me, I inevitably hit the wrong key at times, sending my computer screen into a frenzy of palpitating pixels before the dreaded "error message" pops up. Or perhaps you have been assaulted by some insidious computer virus that unraveled all of the personalized settings, individual applications, and unique modifications. In both instances, if our prior settings are not easily recoverable, then we must go back to the manufacturer's default settings. These are the basic, preprogrammed fundamental operations from which most individuals build. When something goes wrong, the system goes to its default settings.

Similarly, we often find ourselves reacting to personal offenses in ways that seem wired into our basic programming. When something goes wrong in our lives, most of us have a consistent reaction. The offense may be small or only a minor inconvenience, but some people naturally fly off the handle and react as if their mother *and* their grandmother had been insulted! And what seems major to many of us merely rolls off the back of others who just shrug their shoulders and move on. Sometimes people underreact about an offense and allow someone to bulldoze over them when they should have put a stop to the situation as soon as the first spoonful of dirt came flying their way.

Often people who are the most hostile or disappointed when attacked respond that way because they see themselves as the most vulnerable. I know it sounds strange, but I have learned that many times the most unforgiving people remain callous as an attempt to protect their proverbial inner child from further hurt, disappointment, and fear. Others feel so wounded by offenses that they become unwilling to give up the familiar role of victim for the uncertain authenticity of living off-script. If you know that your wheels feel stuck and unable to break free of old grudges, distant regrets, and past injuries, then it's vitally important to examine the mud in which you're stuck! Here are some of the many reasons why people refuse to let go of old issues, forgive their offenders, and move on.

1. Unforgiveness comes when we believe that our future has been taken from us or irreparably damaged.
2. Unforgiveness comes when we believe the betrayal has not been sufficiently atoned.
3. Unforgiveness comes as a defense mode to protect the bruised inner self, which often is hidden from view or even our own awareness.
4. Unforgiveness comes when we feel that we have been deceived in some way and publicly humiliated.
5. Unforgiveness comes when personal trust has been violated.
6. Unforgiveness comes from opportunities lost.
7. Unforgiveness comes when we have been forced to suffer the soul wounds of abuse, neglect, and rejection in silence.

While far from being an exhaustive list, this short catalog may shed light on the portals of entry through which our feelings have come to be mired to a halt. All of us have had moments that we felt these feelings and were hurt to the core.

And yet many people rise above it and move on while others are left immobilized by the wounds that were inflicted, unable to rise above the injury, reliving the incidents over and over in their mind. These prisoners of the past may be wondering why they have not been able to move beyond their emotional quicksand onto solid ground. Others with more traumatic injuries recover and pass them by, all while they are missing the freedom to re-create themselves, revive their relationships, and reclaim job opportunities. Despite their best attempts, they cannot move beyond what has occurred, flailing backward into the same pit of anger, hostility, and rage from which they started.

If you have ever been there, you know that these feelings are incredibly life draining. Anytime you are being controlled by your emotions rather than you controlling them, you are a prisoner without a jail cell. And some remain incarcerated for their entire lives, all while the keys to freedom are dangling within reach.

It's All Relative

You see, no matter how intractable and unmanageable our lack of forgiveness feels, the truth is that we have a choice. Now, before you get upset, please keep in mind that when I say forgiveness is a choice, I don't mean that you can just flip a switch and have the world bloom in animated Technicolor! We will unpack more of what's involved in choosing to forgive in future chapters. But first, we must realize that unforgiveness is a learned behavior.

We do not come here with the propensity to be grudge-bearing

beings. A baby cries one moment and coos the next. Unforgiveness is not present in small children. A child can be chastised
one moment and hug you the next. They can be wrestling on the
playground over who gets to swing first one moment and holding
hands and playing ring-around-the-rosy the next! I have chastised
my children and they were sorely resentful for about a half hour,
but shortly thereafter, their love outweighed the displeasure and
they initiated reconciliation without my prompting.

So if this stubborn, unrelenting anger isn't inherent in us then
how does it become our default setting? In reality, you and I must
realize that those around us teach their method of conflict resolution without always being aware that they are doing it. From the
earliest of our existence, we learn so much about forgiveness, or
the lack thereof, from our family, community, peers, and friends.
Do you ever catch yourself exploding and saying something that
your father always said? Or perhaps silently seething in the moment, just as the women in your family tend to do, even as you're
mentally editing the juicy gossip you will spread about your offender? Take a close look at your family and see if you notice traces
of how they handle stress evident in your own behavior.

My wife always says if you want to know what the parents
think of you, then watch their children's reaction to you. Several
years ago, I realized I was living proof of her wisdom. At that time
I encountered some relatives with whom I had always held reservations. They had always been pleasant enough to me, but I had always kept them at arm's length. I had no previous interaction with
them to cause me to have such reservation. I wasn't sure why I felt
the way I did other than the fact that I knew my mother didn't like
them. I had heard her say so. My dad was leery of a couple of them,
too, and so I didn't trust them, either.

Now, bear in mind my mother has been dead for many years,

but what I learned from her still lives. Many of the things she intentionally taught me were wonderful and life-giving influences, but her method of conflict resolution wasn't intentionally taught. It was one of the things I learned as a child through observation. In retrospect, I realize that my parents' notion of being tough, of not allowing anyone to misuse us, went beyond a healthy defense to the extreme of total dismissal for anyone who had demeaned, disappointed, or deceived us in any way. If my parents found someone in violation of our code of ethics, no matter how great or small their violation, they were condemned without any hope of reprieve.

This way of dismissing people was seen as strength. I hold very few childhood memories of my parents reconciling with people who had disappointed them in some way. More times than not, if you managed to get on their bad side, it was a life sentence with no parole for good behavior. Even if you profusely apologized, my grandmother would still say, "Treat them with a long-handled spoon!" Which meant to remain leery of them permanently if you wanted to avoid a similar state of total damnation!

Family Feud

I would come to realize that many times people hurt you and there's nothing you can do to prevent it. However, in order to release the baggage of unforgiveness, I had to learn on my own how to extend copious amounts of a most precious commodity I found myself needing frequently—mercy. I learned that justice without mercy isn't truly justice at all.

Now, understand that my parents didn't sit down with a chalkboard and pencils and teach me to hold on to anger. It was just that I, like most children, learned from what I saw. While

I certainly observed them handle different conflicts, the overall consistency of their responses formed a deep pattern that became a worldview, a paradigm for dealing with the offenses of others. Without our even realizing it, our learned coping mechanisms often set the tone in our families.

There is a line in *Jumping the Broom,* a movie I coproduced. It comes during a scene where an aristocratic character in the movie named Mr. Watson is having a dispute with his wife. He says to her, "Your family always had a way of responding to problems with sarcasm and that is exactly how you are treating me!" He goes on to say in the heat of their argument, "And frankly, I am getting kind of tired of it." He made the connection between his observations about his in-laws' style of conflict management and its manifestation in how his wife related to him. Perhaps you've experienced similar epiphanies about your own spouse, hearing echoes of his or her parents' voices in the middle of your discussions.

When I married my wife I told her prior to the wedding, "I am not marrying your family and you are not marrying mine!" By starting our own new family, I hoped to prune some of the less desirable branches of both our family trees! Sounds good, doesn't it? Certainly does, but it is totally impossible to achieve. You may not be marrying the entire family, but many of the coping mechanisms from them make their way into your relationship nonetheless!

Most families have a pathology that has been passed down from generation to generation. No one signs a contract or takes an oath, and yet it rolls forward into future generations. It doesn't enter in through DNA nor is it studied in an overt way. It's a covert response we learned as we all adapted to the environment that spawned us. Our parents and grandparents simply acted it out, and the obedient children playing in the corner found themselves listening to the phone conversations, watching the parents who remained silently angry at the dinner table for weeks on end, or missing their best friends with whom they'd fallen out but refused to talk to. Such messages, spoken and unspoken, became our schoolmasters.

And now we are teaching our own children some of the same methods of conflict interaction and stubborn justification that we learned from our elders. Our innocent little children are quietly taking notes that we cannot see. They don't write the notes with pen and paper, but they record it in a far more difficult place to erase. Just as we once did, they record it in their heart!

No doubt my sainted mother didn't create her grudge-holding propensities. She likely saw it demonstrated for her as well. Who knows how far back this habit has been brewing? If we don't model forgiveness, we can't teach it. If we remain angry with our children, spouse, or neighbors we are teaching our young ones that one of the attributes of adulthood is an unwillingness to forgive. If there are no role models for extending mercy, then how do we learn and break the generational strongholds?

Think for a moment about how you've learned, or failed to learn, about what it means to forgive someone. None of us took conflict resolution in school. One can graduate from college and have not one course on how to deal with conflict. Churches tell us what to do, but neither model it nor demonstrate how to accomplish it. In fact, churches are often the most unforgiving of us all! CEOs can have a moral failure, rebound, and run the company. But when our clergy are discovered in a moral failure, they are too often permanently destroyed. In a later chapter, we will explore this tragedy and discuss how the church can be restored to a place for healing, reconciliation, and forgiveness.

So if our academic institutions didn't educate us, and our

moral institutions didn't teach us, then where would we be expected to acquire the skills to release our pain and forgive the perpetrator?

Mood Poisoning

This undercurrent of generational unforgiveness moves silently beneath the surface of the family unit, inevitably grabbing each child and pulling him or her down into the undertow of resentment and prejudice against anyone resembling past offenders. Parents do not see it as harmful; to the contrary, they believe they're providing protection for the bruised. But what one individual did to your grandmother is not cause for you to avoid an entire gender, race, or church denomination of the same kind! In reality, clinging to generational unforgiveness is as foolish as drinking poison and waiting on someone else to die.

It is possible to have evolved circumstantially but remain deeply entrenched in your perspectives. Every progressive opportunity requires some form of extreme adaptation or the opportunity is often forfeited and regression begins. Your gift may carry you into an arena where your character cannot keep you.

Consider that when the Children of Israel were brought out of Egypt, as the Bible says, their oppressor was destroyed and their promises lay before them. God with great power delivered them from their past. However, their murmuring and complaining evidenced that they were struggling to adapt to the very freedom they prayed for. The problem was adaptability. Simply stated, they were out of Egypt but Egypt wasn't out of them. They had a desire for the milk and honey of the Promised Land, but they had an appetite based on four hundred years of living with the leeks and onions of Egypt!

If we want to learn the art of forgiveness, then we have to learn to savor its sweet flavor. Just because the bitter taste in our mouth is familiar does not mean that it is what we truly crave. Old appetites may actually be a case of lingering indigestion from the mood poisoning of the past. We must learn to change our menus if we want to be truly satisfied.

The Scent of Success

Several years ago I witnessed a woman who started working in the inner city with young people who had the education to work in the corporate world but not the social acumen to match their educational expertise. While intelligent, talented, and capable, these young adults could not control their personal issues in a professional environment. When they encountered conflict, their reactions would override their abilities.

In fact, when enraged they reverted to street-style anger, which was their default setting. Their defense mechanisms, nurtured by what they witnessed and experienced growing up in the inner city, formed an emotional land mine, lying dormant like a cancer cell in the body. It was only a matter of time before circumstances ignited trouble.

It was fascinating to have this discussion with her as she had her finger on the pulsebeat of why these highly trained people were often dismissed. They usually thought it was for other reasons, like racism or sexism, but in fact it was a direct result of their reversion to an immature way of handling conflict. They allowed the anger or bitterness that we all feel on the job sometimes to hijack their rational mind and divert their career from one of ascension to one of constant turbulence. The main goal of this woman counseling and coaching them was to retrain the adult person to manage their feelings in a professional manner that would facilitate success rather than constitute an obstacle. She offered them a lifeline as they consistently fell back into the abyss of family dysfunction.

She told me her biggest challenge was getting these young people to recognize the problem with how they handled pressure in the workplace. Their unreasonable outbursts did not seem to be the problem to them because their default setting was the only one they knew. Drama was their only kind of normal. When people grow up around unforgiveness, they see it as acceptable and do not understand the negative impact it has on successful advancement. Their mode of behavior locks them out of opportunities for which they are qualified academically but for which they lack the people skills to fit within the atmosphere of cooperative collaboration.

They perceive unforgiveness as strength and forgiveness as vulnerability, never understanding that forgiveness requires the greater strength and maturity of character. Also they don't seem to realize that their subtle signals of protest made them undesirable for professional workplaces. It wasn't always that they swore and physically fought. But they, like skunks in the forest, secreted signals to all around that they were perturbed. Few who worked with them could regain relationship once conflict was ignited.

Traffic Signals

Recently, when Dr. Howard Hendricks spoke at our marriage seminar, he warned of nonverbal ways that we send messages to people, causing them to respond to us in certain ways. It reminded me of traffic lights behind the eyes. These red-light, green-light, proceed-with-caution signs are often transmitted through our eyes and send signals we're not aware are being sent. Even when our lips say the right words, it is possible that our body language sends out a message of hidden anger lurking just below our veneer of political correctness.

The physiology of this process fascinates me, and I was intrigued to learn that the pupils dilate when the amygdala opens. An almond-shaped mass located deep within the temporal lobe of the brain, the amygdala helps regulate many of our emotions and motivations, particularly those related to survival. The amygdala is involved in the processing of emotions such as fear, anger, and pleasure. One of the ways it signals these fight-or-flight emotions is through the dilation of our pupils, which in turn causes those around us to sense safety or danger depending on how they regard our pupils. This is not consciously done by either person, but is a biological reaction to a psychological sense of hostility or comfort.

These signals cause those around us to sense safety or agitation. Without even realizing it, we may be thwarting our chances of reconciliation as we subconsciously employ our body's natural defense mechanisms. Or we may be reacting to someone else's nonverbal signs of hostility. Think if you will of animals who can sense when the master is displeased and often will not approach him as they detect a sense of agitation that threatens them and makes them flee or be wary. It is a glare versus a gaze. If you are glaring at me, it sends a signal out that makes me know to be defensive, as we have conflict.

This is a normal physiological tendency. However, when we allow these subconscious signals to remain as a part of our norm without learning how to drop those defenses and seek solutions, we subtly alienate others as well as model it for our children. Toddlers as well as teens know how to read the unspoken messages sent when Mom raises her eyebrow toward Dad, or when Dad rolls his eyes while on the phone with someone he pretends to respect. These silent weapons of destruction shatter the atmosphere at work, at home, or at play.

Now, it isn't likely that we can control these normal physiological reactions, but that isn't our goal. I mention them simply to emphasize how these clues are left behind as evidence to how we really feel about those with whom we interact. Too often we remain ill at ease with people with whom we should have resolved our issues and normalized the atmosphere.

So if we cannot control our bodies' responses to the emotions of unforgiveness, then how do we overcome these propensities? I am glad you asked. In order to begin this process, we must see the issue, and not the individual, as the enemy. It is the conflict we want to resolve and not the person we want to defeat. If we can begin to train ourselves to attack the issue and not the individual, we become far more productive and break the inherited, atmospheric cycle that robs us of the opportunities for advancement before us.

Our goal is to mature to the degree that we rise above the temporary discomfort triggered when someone offends us or gets in our way with an agenda at variance with our own. If we had grown up in an environment of forgiveness and reconciliation, then we wouldn't be so quick to remain in a state of heightened alert. Every issue isn't a level-orange situation, and discerning how we respond is a part of maturity that must be employed in order to maximize our growth opportunities.

Law of the Jungle

Now that we understand how these reactions originated, both physiologically and experientially, we must begin to manage them so that we can move forward. No longer will we allow unhealthy patterns that were subconsciously ingrained subvert the goals of a peaceful, harmonious atmosphere. If we allow ourselves to remain stuck, then we will only end up with others who are also immobilized, all while those with full tanks and well-tuned engines accelerate toward their goals. The Bible says that those who live by the sword will also die by it. In short, if we don't unlearn these behaviors, then ultimately we will only attract others with similar points of reference.

Consider how entire communities turn into ghettos filled with violence, and yet no one seems willing to move out and make their home in a safer, more peaceful environment. While no one holds residents hostage to their community, they eventually accept violence on their doorstep and street crime as normal. They may still complain but they do not take action to change their circumstances. Like mice trained to stay in the cage with an open door, they remain in place as if they are unable to move through the door to freedom. But I am here to say you can escape the training of your past and evolve into the person you were meant to be.

Several years ago I was on safari in South Africa and had a very knowledgeable guide lead me through the jungle. I was amazed at how many different species with varying strengths coexisted in the same jungle. As we traveled through the bush, I saw ferocious lions, deadly snakes, giant giraffes, and elegant gazelles—all different creatures that existed in this same dangerous atmosphere. But I realized that they are able to do so because they understand the unspoken rules of their jungle.

I thought to myself, "Isn't it odd that you could take them out of the wild jungle with its many threats and put them in the zoo, where supposedly all their needs are met, and yet they might die?" Actually, every arena is a jungle. But your survival depends on how well you understand and adapt to the rules of that new jungle. The single person who wants a spouse has to adapt to the marriage jungle. The secular person has to adapt to a spiritual jungle. The entrepreneur has to adapt to the corporate jungle. Each arena of life has predators, spectators, and dangers to be discerned. If we are to advance beyond the jungle we were born in, then we must adapt to the jungle we are called to.

Several years ago while on the Rock of Gibraltar my guide told me that the monkeys born on the top of the rock used to be born with tails as most monkeys are. However, during certain climate changes the top of the rock consistently became so bitter cold that their tails would freeze and fall off. Over time and many generations, new monkeys were born without tails. They naturally and organically adapted to their new environment in which having a tail was a painful liability.

People who have savage anger in civilized environments haven't adapted yet to the new jungle. They must recognize that what may have once allowed them to survive now holds them back and threatens their existence in their new environment.

I was fascinated during the 2008 presidential election when President Obama made his speech about race in America. He asserted that the seemingly hostile remarks by his former pastor were age related. He said, "For the men and women of Reverend Wright's generation, the memories of humiliation and doubt and fear have not gone away; nor has the anger and the bitterness of those years. That anger may not get expressed in public, in front of white coworkers or white friends. But it does find voice in the barbershop or around the kitchen table."

I so agree with his observation. You see, our parents survived the atrocities of Jim Crow and the beating and jailing associated with that time. It is now very difficult for them to adapt to this present time when racism still exists only without wearing sheets! I certainly know we have more work to do, but I also understand that this is a different kind of jungle and the anger that past generations hold is counterproductive to the new jungle we are in!

There will be many issues to arise whereby we have to take justifiable issue. Our right to be displeased isn't the challenge here. Our need to respond is without question more than a need; it is a necessity. However, we must grow beyond past responses and lingering displeasure. We no longer need to allow an incident to turn into an all-out war! If we don't learn how to respond and express our disagreement without becoming vitriolic and retaliatory, we will regress back into the old jungle whose laws we imitate and lose the precious gift of dwelling in a new situation with a new attitude.

At the end of the day, what we must realize is that we may have very well adopted a response from a previous generation that doesn't fit the environment we were blessed by them to inherit. Often our response mechanisms are a result of what we saw around us. Now through education, opportunity, technology, and life itself we have been placed in a completely different environment. If we do not allow ourselves to evolve and seize the new knowledge, tools, and abilities at our disposal, then we risk regressing to an existence mediocre at best. While we may have been subtly conditioned to respond by the environment from which we came, we are no longer those same people living in that same environment.

Like the Gibraltar monkeys who evolved away from producing a tail that didn't fit their new surroundings, all of us have a chance to change our response to reflect our contemporary context. Today as you purpose in your heart that you don't want to respond to your present out of the pain of your past, you are one step closer to stepping into your future with newfound freedom. Never lose sight of the valuable lessons and wisdom from your parents and ancestors. If nothing else, we have learned the art of survival or we wouldn't even be here. But as my grandmother would say about eating a fresh catch of fish that my uncle brought home: "Eat the meat and leave the bones behind!"

four
Silence Doesn't Mean Consent

As we forge deeper into this issue of forgiveness, we must be prepared to open up and discuss things that bother us before they escalate to a crisis level. We must examine our struggles with forgiveness in which there are not overt offenses or blatant betrayals. I'm convinced that seeds of resentment take root in the silent frustrations that never get discussed. Other people cannot read our minds—or our palms!—and that is why we have tongues to speak.

If we don't learn to communicate honestly and transparently, the silent frustration of our unmet expectations will poison us with their toxicity and no one else knows. I'm convinced that there are painful emotional wounds that we suppress so deeply we don't even discuss them with ourselves. Silent frustration leads to the secret seething that works inside of us to pollute and destroy what is most important to us.

Or consider the unspoken resentments and hidden anger

festering in the hearts of the people we love, all while we think everything is fine based on their false sense of well-being. Then the person reaches their secret boiling point one too many times and suddenly explodes into a scalding volcano of vitriolic emotional lava, engulfing your relationship in a conflagration that you could never have imagined. In the mega-gigabyte, nanosecond world of Facebook, Twitter, and texting, I fear that the real essence of communication can sometimes get lost among the tweets and the pixels. The relentless pace of our lives often reinforces the assumptions we make based on silence, lurking dormant below the surface of our cheerful responses of "I'm fine—how are you?" Before we know it, the germs of discontent have multiplied into a debilitating virus that jeopardizes our relationships and hurts our productivity and creativity.

Preventive Maintenance

Often people so honor or respect us that they smother discontentment to appear congenial. This kind of deception is often well meaning but can really rob us of a real fighting chance at a better atmosphere at home and at work. Just because a person shows up at work and completes basic assignments doesn't ensure that they are really fulfilled in the workplace. I have seen time and time again frustration imitate cancer and silently engulf people who avoid confrontation to the point of becoming martyrs simply because they lack the courage or the skills to be forthcoming about little areas of discontentment. Then, before you ever saw it coming, you have lost an excellent team member to the silent progression of a discontentment that could have been avoided by communicating about a few small things long before they became major issues.

We tend to live our lives like a mechanic who only greases the squeaky wheel without checking the vital parts of the engine under the hood. He figures that if the car still starts then everything must be fine with the engine, not bothering to check the vital fluids of oil, transmission fluid, coolant, and of course, gasoline. Relationships are the one place where the old saying "If it ain't broke, don't fix it" is bad advice. Waiting until the car stalls to check the engine may be too late. What could have been prevented with routine maintenance has evolved into a problem annihilating the entire engine.

There is wisdom and proactive power in doing preventive maintenance on the car, on the staff, on the family, and all else we have that's dear. They can be in trouble and never squeak at all! Preventive maintenance is never a waste of time but is more aptly a wise way of preventing molehills from becoming mountains. That is why I don't take on more friendships than I can handle. It's not fair to me or to the other person if we cannot commit at even a basic level to doing the necessary requirements for cooperative communication. Relationships require maintenance. There's an investment of time, energy, and transparency that cannot be taken for granted.

If you have a husband, he will require maintenance. If you have a dog, he will require trips to the vet and walking and watering. If you have a goldfish, you have to change the tank and feed the fish. The more you have the more time you must budget not just for acquisition but also for maintenance. Don't take on more than you are willing to take care of. Count the cost of the relational investment and commit to the necessary maintenance before you lose the opportunity to know the other person.

Learn to spot early warning signs that unspoken tension is accumulating. The sooner you nip it in the bud, the less likely you are to have an offense growing in the office, the church, or your home that assaults your relationship essentials. If we want to learn to swim in the sea of forgiveness, then we must not drift to the surface and assume that everything's fine because the water's calm around us. We must be willing to dive below the surface and check the temperature, the current, and the incoming tide on a regular basis. We can never assume that silence is consent when it comes to dealing with people.

An Affair to Remember

Yes, the silent messages and imaginary conversations in any relationship must be addressed constructively or else they will manifest themselves in a destructive flood that threatens everything in its path. I'm reminded of a couple who recently came to me in a marital rift that threatened to destroy their once blissful union. By the time most people seek counseling, they are generally in serious trouble and this case was no exception. What had once been a small mole on the face of their relationship had now grown into a stage-four cancer threatening all that they knew and once held so dear.

The wife was hurt and furious, and with good reason. Her husband had been caught in a very compromising situation with another woman. His story added new meaning to the old adage about being caught with your pants down. He literally had been caught with his Fruit of the Looms wrapped around his ankles, and man oh man was his wife angry!

As they shared their story, he was in tears. And even though this incident had happened almost a year before, it seemed clear that she seemed unable to find the strength to forgive him and lacked the resolve to move on. Unfortunately, being stuck between leaving and staying is a nowhere-land position that many couples may exist in for years. Just because people stay together doesn't mean they are happily married. This woman had not left her husband, but it was clear that she wasn't present in their marriage, either.

It took me a while to get to the bottom of it, and I never would have been able to do so had I not separated them in my office so I could move beyond the who-done-me-wrong song and cut to the chase. Each of them was a quality person, and I wanted to get to the real nitty-gritty of the underlying cause of the infidelity. I could tell that he was an honorable man who had done a dishonorable thing. He was grieved and embarrassed and when I got him by himself I began to ask the kind of probing questions that exhumed the real source of the conflict.

On the surface it seemed that she was having trouble forgiving him. I could certainly understand why. After all he had acted despicably and his selfish actions had opened up every insecurity she had fought so hard to submerge. She was feeling inadequate about things he really wasn't focused on. Their conflict wasn't about stretch marks or bad hair days. But every little flaw she noticed in herself had her screaming at him, repeatedly accusing him of more indiscretions. But I know that infidelity is often more about the perpetrator than it is about the victim.

He had violated his oath to her, and she was hurt to the core. He had asked her to forgive him, and she had said that she did even as it was clear to them both that she had not. His behavior had unleashed all the zombies from her past. Her thought life had come to resemble *Night of the Living Dead,* her imagination taunting her with limitless possibilities and her memories haunting her with painful images. Emotionally exhausted from fighting all the ghosts, she now was trying to find a place of real forgiveness despite her open wounds.

Curiously enough, however, when I dug down to the root of the problem, he harbored more unforgiveness than his wife did! And to make it even worse, it was a resentment that his wife didn't even know he had harbored long before the infidelity transpired. I knew if we didn't uncover the root cause the relationship was doomed. He suffered from unforgiveness long before she did and was actually respectfully angry toward her. Did you get that— *respectfully* angry? Because he buried it beneath his polite veneer, a growing cancer had erupted between them that could have been completely avoided!

Adjusting the Thermostat

Now, I am asking you to understand that forgiveness isn't just needed when violation occurs. It is also needed when intimacy is denied, needs aren't met, or honest communication has waned. The husband was trapped in a relationship that was lukewarm sexually and to some degree emotionally. Now, lukewarm works when both of you like that temperature. But when one of you is operating at 212 degrees Fahrenheit and the other is happy at 92 you can have real problems! One of you is happy with a temperature that's making the other nauseous!

As a young man, he had entered the marriage expecting his wife to be as sexually "in touch" with herself as she was vibrant and attentive in all the other ways that he needed. He confided that she had been much more in touch with herself before they were married, freer and less inhibited. Yes, the sexual relationship had started before the wedding cake was cut. But the bigger problem is that he expected to marry the woman he dated but now secretly felt betrayed once she lapsed back into what was for her a normal temperature of life. I don't think she understood that adding someone in your life means you can't go back to normal. I don't think he realized that the person you date will not be identical to the one you marry. You have to recalibrate to a new normal.

But once they were married the boiling pot had cooled to a simmer, and he was annoyed—not because she didn't have what he needed, which would be understandable, but because she had revealed her capacity for the kind of passion he craved when they were dating. Years down the road, however, he found his resentment multiplying exponentially. With life and responsibilities, they had not invested into each other properly, had not communicated openly, and he was secretly frustrated and she wasn't even aware.

Now, no one can excavate out of you what isn't buried inside of you. But his anger was rooted in the fact that he felt she was denying him. He described it as bait and switch, the marketing term used when a store lures you in with the promise of purchasing an outrageously low-priced product that they already know they have in short supply, and then offers you a higher-priced item in its place. He thought she was denying him the deep parts of her that she had advertised. He didn't take into account that the distractions of life had left her unfocused on the luxury of self-awareness. They were both so busy they lived in a constant perpetual survival mode until they themselves were submerged beneath the current of the life they had built together.

Excavating the Truth

Perhaps it was how good of a mother and companion his wife was in other ways that convinced this man to bite the bullet on the sexual part of their lives and bury how he really felt. Maybe it was the fact that he loved someone that he also resented. His emotions were complicated in part because they lacked the ventilation that occurs when we open up and speak honestly. Now, to be sure, the infidelity was not her fault. He could've said no to the temptation. He could have dug inside of himself and sought counseling. He was and is responsible for his decisions and his actions.

However, as I talked to him I began to unravel a relationship where he had never given her an honest picture of his heart and what he needed from her beyond dinner on the table and diapers for the children. They both had been duped by the silence that had engulfed them into a false sense of security and missed the maintenance that having more of anything requires. He shared how she had seemed occasionally engaged in their intimate life together, but for the most part was contented by a very basic awareness of their physical love even as she occasionally still flashed glimpses of the deeper passion within her. "It" was as important to him as you could imagine, but he hid his needs and faked his compliance while lying in bed wishing for the woman he thought he had married. She didn't understand that "it" and "him" were inextricably connected.

He never discussed with her the fact that he often lay in bed feeling depressed by what she thought was a satisfactory level of intimacy. He never told her that her allowing him to see how she could or would be if she were more open was like dangling a piece of meat just beyond his reach, leaving him hungrier and silently frustrated. Rather than taking the risk to unveil his real longings and having frank discussions about what his needs were, he, how shall we say, "went along to get along." He foolishly attempted to treat his discontentment with pornography, which then eventually progressed into an affair with a woman he didn't even love to protect a woman he said he truly did love. He didn't seem to realize that protecting her feelings led him to breaking her heart. Knowing that many women divorce never knowing what really caused the breach between them because it is so hard to get men to talk, I encouraged him to be open and honest with her regardless of the outcome.

Submit to the Mission

Now, many marriages don't survive such trauma, and those that do often take several stages to heal. There is a term used to describe people who have given and given until they have nothing else left to give: "donor fatigue." Many times people who have fought cancer together or fought through the death of a loved one, simply split after all has been said and done because they have spent so much energy in the short run that they have nothing else emotionally to contribute for the happily-ever-after part. They have exhausted the love budget and suffer from donor fatigue. The toll of constant withdrawals with no deposits leaves the equity depleted and the balance plummets until the bottom line shrinks to zero. Such a deficit often bankrupts the relationship. Those that do succeed do so because people involved have learned the art of loving above the offense. They simply outlove the injury and build on that equity that has been accrued through years of relationship or the enormity of unused inventory of affection so that they can transcend the offense. And though the world, and often the media, criticizes those who stay (I believe in part to avoid having to look at their own failed relationships), the reality is we see couples every day who sustain a Hillary Clinton kind of personal injury and find a way to maintain their dignity and to love beyond the offense.

In the case with my couple in counseling, they both wanted

the marriage to work. This desire superseded their personal agendas and injured egos. In order to transition into a new season of healing and rebuilding trust, they both had to find a place of submission. Consider what that word "submission" really means; literally you must submit to the mission. It means that we agree that the "we" of the relationship is more important than the "me" of it. And both of us are willing to submit to the mission of "us."

When your dream life together is still so important to you that you are both willing to spend more to cover the overdraft than the offense costs, then you are submitting to the mission. This can only be done when the mission supersedes the misdeeds. Trust has to be rebuilt over time and often more time than the perpetrator expects.

Many people in the workplace have a personal agenda but no commitment to the mission of the corporation. They want to be a superstar at the office or go after the promotion, but they don't buy into the team concept and inevitably fail to understand that they were hired to enhance the team and not compete with the team. Ultimately, I'm afraid it all comes down to selfishness, and as harsh as that word sounds, we'd better identify it or we can't correct it. If you don't believe in the power of a team, then start a sole proprietorship and work on your dream solely and exclusively. If you don't believe in the team, don't get married. Because if you do, you have to give up on some of the "me" of it all for the "we" of it all!

Loving Above the Offense

Likewise when our own needs supersede the importance of our collective mission, no one submits to the mission and each goes his own way. I see it happen in churches, resulting in splits; in marriages, resulting in divorce; and in families, where mother and daughter or father and son stop speaking for years. All too often the relationship deteriorates beyond repair because the individuals are emotionally bankrupt with nothing left to sacrifice!

The couple I counseled dug in deep and agreed to love above the offense and submit to the mission of their marriage. Love has its work cut out for it when an offense is deep. But love never fails. Blaming will fail, revenge will fail, but love never fails!

So I encouraged them to find ways to communicate information that isn't always polite or flattering to protect the mission that was very important to them both. Hiding doesn't help intimacy; it destroys it. I wanted this man to understand that her sexual indifference wasn't a locked door but merely a closed door that could be reopened. Lord, have mercy, it wasn't easy and sometimes opening up brought tears and rage from them both. I shared with them the importance of wrapping what is hard to hear in what is good to hear. It is kind of like putting honey on a spoon with castor oil!

Their honest heart communication had to include how wonderful she was and how much he loved her and how he longed to be able to access her more fully and what he needed to do to create an atmosphere that made her feel safe to unleash what she had only allowed him snippets of in the past. He had to learn that it isn't what you say but how you say it. He quickly began to realize that his silence wasn't golden but merely the tinfoil that had wrapped the entire circumference of his infidelity. Some men, and some women for that matter, find it difficult to be open and honest about who they really are even to those they truly love.

Others don't know themselves well enough to explain themselves. They are like blind people at an art show or like the hearing impaired attending an opera. They don't have the skills to articulate or appreciate the moment until it is almost gone. This presents an extra obstacle—not an insurmountable one, but one nonetheless that must be addressed if the relationship is to be repaired and restored. New skills must be learned. Default habits must be unlearned and abandoned. Ways of behaving that might have once been effective or even productive may now be defunct and obsolete.

Sadly this man took a wrong turn and fell into the shortcuts so pervasive among men. He found himself relating to someone he didn't want under the guise of protecting someone that he really wanted. Fortunately, they both were enlightened and repented to God and to each other and began to learn the tools of communication necessary to avoid further compromise. I was so relieved because many times such lethal behavior doesn't have a happy ending; thankfully, this time it did. They realized at the end of the blame game that the real culprit wasn't him or her but the tumor of silence that was allowed to rob them of what they now fought to rebuild.

It isn't enough to tell people to communicate. Most find it easier to criticize and complain than to reveal the vulnerability of need and expectations. I began to think of how so many couples end up fighting about the bills, which have nothing to do with the source of either's frustration. My prayer has become, "Lord, teach us how to say what we mean even when it risks making one another temporarily uncomfortable."

This power of the truth isn't relegated to marriage alone. The essence of authenticity and honest communication is relative to every area of life in which the stakes are high and we need so desperately to win. It is important in parenting to break the silence or risk losing the child. Yes, we need to speak but also to listen. To ask questions and not allow assumptions to leave you with false information that eats away the love between you. Surely as an employer, I have learned that people quit a job many times long before they resign. They endure things that could easily be discussed and remedied but instead they seethe until their discontent rages like an inferno. In short, what you don't know can hurt you. And it can also hurt those around you.

Now, before you crucify him with a coat hanger, examine yourself. How often have you said you liked something you didn't? How many times have you allowed your need to be seen as a good guy or girl to overcome your need to be transparent and forthcoming? People lie with their lips open as well as with their lips closed all the time. The truth evaporates and both souls remain parched with only a mirage, the illusion of an oasis, between them.

Speaking Truth in Love

> "Instead, speaking the truth in love, we will grow to become in every respect the mature body of him who is the head, that is, Christ."
>
> *(Ephesians 4:15, NIV)*

The consequences of silence often emerge long after the relationship crumbles, like the discovery of termites in a home that looked beautiful and sturdy before it simply collapsed one day. I wish I had a dollar for every time I have seen a deal lost that could have been negotiated to resolution if people would just have learned to speak up. How many times do you find yourself walking away from a failed deal secretly wondering what would have made the deal work? The point gets lost in the emotions and anger wins over reason. And when it does, we all suffer the consequences.

Staff members fighting for power, not trusting the people who you work with, destroys so much potential and possibility. Confronting the issue as the problem rather than attacking the person is so much more effective. No one likes being attacked, but if you can get the other person to help you attack a common problem, you are both far better served.

The challenge is to create an atmosphere where people can be transparent, enhancing everyone's productivity and building team bonds that last beyond the grave. Yes, you may bully them into silence or intimidate them into temporary compliance, but the cancer of conflict that appears to have gone into remission will surely resurrect again and again until you create a way for someone to say what they feel even if what they feel isn't what you want to hear!

Lord, help us share with overbearing bosses, fast-talking salesmen, distracted fathers, and angry verbal wives that winning the battle in the argument doesn't mean you have won the war. Just because you outtalk someone and a person grows quiet doesn't mean that the silence is a sign of your victory. Often just the contrary. In order to negotiate the win-win deal that we want in every arena of our lives, we have to run the risk of being honest with those we want and need to be involved with, whatever the relationship may be.

Everyone involved must have a voice that isn't encumbered or oppressed. Believe me, there are a lot of ways to be talked into silence. Religious people do it all the time. They use the faith they have to intimidate the person they have silenced with scriptures, rules, and regulations. Outspoken people shush slow talkers and speed-talk them into a gradual, brooding silence that deadens the love and erects the bitterness. All of this can be grown inside the other person without one further word being uttered.

Intimidation can be the culprit, or sometimes it isn't the intimidation of the one person but the insecurity of the other that leads to such a drastic turn of events. Let's face it: Many people do not have the tools they need to have the discussion they long for.

Talking Points

The couple that I counseled learned what every CEO must learn if he or she is going to create an atmosphere that causes a company to grow. You must create an atmosphere where people can say what they need to say and not just what you want to hear. If you are going to benefit from the people you employ you can't intimidate them into silence and miss the chance to make the team more effective. You may agree to compromise on the final solutions but no one wins when one of you must be a mute in order for the other one to be happy.

If you are serious about fixing things at work, at home, or at church, you must be willing to listen even if the person is stumbling to communicate, or touches a nerve you don't like. Love grows when we offer to each person a voice. How can you have loyalty in a work situation that denies input? What you will see is a growing resentment and I am trying to make you understand that these issues don't show symptoms until the relationship is in the final stages of frustration, and some of the damage can be fatal to the mission.

Here are eight antioxidants you can use to prevent the silent erosion that destroys those you need.

1. Develop the art of listening with an unconditional ear.
2. Try to put yourself in the position of the person who has a frustration that needs attention.
3. Understand that when a person says they don't like what you did, it doesn't mean they don't like you.

4. Work toward the goal of a mutually acceptable settlement rather than selfishly ignoring their plea and defending your position.

5. Reward any behavior that is an improvement in meeting the needs you have discussed.

6. Reserve time to check up on the people that are critical to your long-term goals.

7. Don't chastise people for having different needs from your own or perspectives that you haven't considered.

8. Attack the problem and not the individual.

These steps will help avoid many calamities just by providing a model to correct the problems before they occur. Implementing them before there is a crisis may save money for the company or connectivity for the couple. So whether you are trying to work through a problem with your maturing children (whom you raised, incidentally, to have an opinion and yet don't want to hear it when they do), or with your spouse (who you may believe needs to learn to see what you have already discovered, when it's the other way around), or with your work team, make sure you bring the real skills of forgiveness management to the table. It will endear you to your staff and create a loyalty that is priceless. And they may save you from the disgrace of driving a desperate person away from you who wants to be with you but, left alone, may do foolish things to avoid the risk of your wrath because they can't talk to you.

Whoever said silence was golden hadn't heard of fool's gold! As we continue to move through this important subject, you may find yourself with homework to do. You may need to forgive someone who wasn't sensitive to a need you weren't effective at communicating. You may need to forgive someone whose narcissistic attitude didn't make provisions for you having an opinion. You may have to fight off your normal need to defend yourself so you can hear what the other one is trying to say.

The good news is that these tools can help you avoid a court-room from being the first time you are forced to really hear what the other side has been repeatedly saying. This information I am sharing in this book is far more affordable than the consequences of not getting the tools that give voice to concerns before they become cancers. Silence isn't golden and it surely doesn't mean consent, so start practicing the art of communication. Public speaking is far less valuable than private speech so practice your craft at home and at work where you have so much to gain and so very much to lose.

five

The Power of a Pure Heart

Recorded in the Bible is a sermon Jesus delivered called the Beatitudes. During his delivery of these pearls of wisdom, he reveals one that I believe is essential as we continue exploring our healing journey to forgiveness. Jesus says, "Blessed are the pure in heart, for they shall see God" (Matthew 5:8, NIV). He indicates in this statement the relationship between the status of our heart's condition and our ability to experience the divine. Jesus basically tells us the secret to knowing God is spiritual housecleaning, realizing the importance of keeping your inner being free from clutter and debris.

Understand that the heart spoken of here isn't the one beating in your chest but is the core of your essence, your inner self, or your spirit. The term "pure" in this passage points to a term associated with catharsis, the removal of a blockage in order to restore freedom of movement. Now, if blockage of your physical heart is potentially lethal, so, too, is the clutter that can contaminate the valves and ventricles of your inner heart. The implication isn't that you can avoid experiencing such blockage, for as we have discussed offenses are to be expected. Instead, Jesus's statement suggests that some people do not allow the offense to become plaque in the arteries of their creative inner being. Without life-threatening, soul-choking constriction in their heart, these people experience the joy and freedom of an intimate relationship with their Creator. These people who free themselves from long-term emotional debilitation find themselves more blessed, more productive, and much more grounded than those who become blocked by incidents, tragedies, and injustices.

When you cling to past offenses, they cling to your heart and shorten your peaceful performance level by preventing you from exercising the ability to release the hurts and move on. No matter which soul-CPR method you employ, whether it be counseling, self-evaluation, or healthy confrontation, forgiveness is the gift you give yourself so that you can move forward. Rather than becoming stuck and forever tied to an adverse moment that you're constantly rehearsing, reliving, and resuffering, you can utilize forgiveness as a catheter to your heart. Just as a medical catheter drains a physical part of toxic waste and flushes it out of the body, forgiveness siphons the toxic emotions away from the core of our being.

You see, in order to survive and forgive there must be a component of catharsis, a deep cleansing of the soul. Anytime there is emotional stagnancy, your inner health is jeopardized. Lingering issues left without resolution can become lethal to your well-being and block the blessings of creativity, opportunity, and openness to new experiences.

Often the process begins by confronting the truth within

yourself, admitting that you are stuck in a state of reliving or rehearsing what you need to remove and release. You gain nothing by holding your offender as a hostage of your rage, demanding a ransom that they are often incapable of paying. Because in actuality, the only person you're holding hostage is yourself, and you are the only one who can ransom yourself through the power of forgiveness.

Smoke Alarms

Please understand that I am not saying that a person shouldn't be angry in the wake of an assault by an offender. I realize that the combination of a book on forgiveness and its author being clergy might lead you to believe that this is a gentle guide to becoming a Pollyanna-type person who skips through the tulips, smiling and singing, joyfully turning her other cheek and blessing the person who just slapped her the first time! Nothing could be further from the truth. Channeled in a constructive direction, anger can be an incredible asset and a powerful catalyst to catharsis.

I come from generations of people who are outspoken, opinionated, and outright hostile if provoked. I haven't always valued this family trait, but I have come to learn that forgiveness doesn't rob you of power or require anger to disappear. Anger can often provide focus, energy, and determination as you examine the situation and the offense incurred. However, your anger must not be allowed to hijack your journey by locking reason in the trunk!

While you don't want anger driving your decisions and treatment of people, it is not to be discarded as an evil. There is such a thing as healthy anger. In fact, often when people lose their will to live, it's clear they have also lost the ability to be provoked and outraged. Foremost, anger sounds an alarm that you care about something or someone, even if it is just yourself! Like a smoke alarm signaling the presence of a fire that could destroy your home, our anger calls our attention to an issue that we cannot ignore if we want to survive.

Often anger helps us to confront what we would otherwise ignore. Occasionally, I hear people teach others to simply move on from an offense and forget it. But the truth of the matter is that it's difficult to move on when you haven't had your say. The lack of closure can become a sticking point that keeps you attached to an incident from which you need to be free.

You can't overcome what you will not confront. And we seldom confront what hasn't in some way angered us or given us some level of angst! I believe it is important that you do not approach forgiveness as being a whitewashed, fictitious representation of who and how you are. It takes courage to confront issues and wisdom to resolve them. Some people have the anger to confront but lack the wisdom to move beyond their initial emotion and produce a productive resolution. Anger is often the catalyst that makes you confront everything from weight gain to being overlooked for a promotion. Like all vehicles, you do have to watch where it takes you. If you have the kind of anger that makes you hurt people, damage your own property, or give up your position in life, then your vehicle is out of control. But let's not trash the Chevy just because it needs a tune-up!

You came fully loaded from the manufacturer with anger under the hood so that you could use it and not so that it can use you. Like the computer warning system on your dashboard, anger alerts you to some area that requires immediate attention. Anger isn't a gift you should shun; you just have to be careful how you unwrap it.

It took me a while to learn how to harness the fuel of it and make it constructive and not destructive. Between my mother, who always had a tendency to speak her mind, and my father, who had a tendency to respond to her frankness with the tactics of a terrorist, it could really get to be quite dramatic in my house when I was a child. It was a drama that I never wanted to see repeated in my own life.

Consequently, both my wife and I decided that when we had nothing left but that level of rage, we would exit off the next ramp and stay off the highway for a while. That kind of anger-based interaction was not what either of us wanted or would allow. So we both had a tendency to avoid saying or doing anything that would take us to the limit of our emotional composure. While it often worked and allowed us to cool down, we both soon learned that there are times that manners and etiquette have to be sacrificed on the altar of telling the truth and keeping it real!

I had to learn that anger in and of itself is not the negative, always destructive force that I first assumed. It's just a matter of what I do with my anger, where I channel its very combustible energy. Anger is a God-given emotion that if managed correctly can be of huge benefit. A little righteous indignation is a real blessing and can help you to find a place of restoration and peace. If Jesus got angry and used it to set the temple in order (see Mark 11:15–19), then you and I must understand that there are some things within us and around us that we will not correct if we aren't angry about them. What is going on in your temple, your life, and your home that exists solely because you have become docile in an area that you need to confront?

Anger properly allocated can do a lot to ease the torment of a boundary that has been disrespected. Though it isn't as romantic as affection nor as politically correct as politeness, it does help to erase the mask of stoic pretension and show where we stand on issues that are dear to us. Anger is a part of passion that generally is a sign that we still care. Own your anger and stop being in denial. When I see someone display anger, at the very least, I know that something still matters to them (what really alarms me is when I see a person void of response!). To assist you in rethinking how your anger can be used constructively, consider some of its positive qualities, none of which emerge from indifference.

1. Anger makes people tell their truth. It may not be the full truth of the matter, but it is certainly their truth.
2. Anger sets boundaries and lets those around us know where the lines are. Just as an invisible fence creates a low-voltage jolt to remind dogs of the limits of their play area, a little anger also lets others know where your limits are.
3. Anger releases energy. It is the fuel that kick-starts our adrenaline to help us tackle challenges that we might not have had the energy to complete had our anger not been ignited.
4. Anger gives courage. It often helps us to confront what we otherwise would suppress, ignore, or deny. Anger helps us overcome propriety, politeness, and pretense.

As we continue to unleash the power of forgiveness, you must understand that I am not trying to give you an emotional makeover and turn you into a passive, understated statue, standing lifeless in the center of your world like a mannequin in a department store window. No indeed, forgiveness is about embracing yourself and loving all parts of yourself, including emotions such as anger. It simply has to be managed and focused, not discarded or suppressed. Like the flame in one of my grandmother's old oil lamps, you want your anger to provide illumination, not the soot that would often blacken the lamp because the wick was turned up too high! Your blazing rage will block your vision and cause you to perceive things incorrectly. That is why professional boxers avoid anger when they fight. Rage diminishes judgment, and consequently good opportunities are missed because of the soot attached to anger gone wild!

Explosive Dangerous

Just as we find many useable energy sources in this world that are productive only when they are harnessed and handled with care, anger operates in a similar fashion. Once we understand the purpose and power of anger, then we must examine the potential dangers of anger. A nuclear power plant can produce billions of kilowatts of energy, but a nuclear bomb can also devastate half a continent in a mushroom cloud explosion, leaving radioactive waste that poisons every living thing around it for generations.

As we have seen, the first step is often simply to identify anger for what it is. A friend of mine has a small wooden crate on the oak desk in his office. Printed on the side of the crate in faded letters are the words EXPLOSIVE DANGEROUS. When I asked my friend about it, he told me that it was his inbox! I laughed and then he explained what it really was—an old shipping crate for sticks of dynamite! All of us know that dynamite is dangerous, but what makes anger so powerful is that it wears many disguises.

Yes, anger can shroud itself in many costumes. You may be thinking, "Well, I am not angry," and perhaps you aren't. But before you skip over this section, understand that anger doesn't always ignite a head-pounding, eye-twitching rage that makes you throw objects across the room with the velocity of a missile. No, there is that slow-burning, deeply silent, brooding anger that is far less obvious but just as lethal if not more so because of its stealth.

Or what of that self-effacing, humble suit of false modesty that often hides a heart that is deeply resentful and full of the loathing of self and others? The one I like the best is the subtle anger that dresses in polite camouflage apparel, acting as if it has no inner conflict but casually revealing itself through humor, sarcasm, or jokes at others' expense.

Yes, outwardly polite, nice people have been known to come home with a pistol and murder entire households. You've probably heard the term "going postal," which refers to an individual in the workplace suddenly losing his normally calm demeanor and exploding in a fit of deadly rage. Everyone who worked with them thought they were completely fine, but inwardly they harbored resentment that infected their reasoning and in the end caused them to hurt themselves and others. Sadly enough, this phenomenon happens more and more frequently, and not just in post offices but in ministries, businesses, homes, and marriages around the world.

Jump the Tracks

Anger begins to lose its constructive power when it jumps the tracks of reason. As we've seen, this volatile emotion should serve as a fuse lighter to motivate you to remove obstacles that are impeding your greatness and survival. However, when anger stays too long it comes out in destructive emotional patterns that can range from eating disorders to domestic abuse to bitterness. God himself didn't tell us not to be angry; rather he told us to be angry and sin not (Ephesians 4:26, KJV). Feeling angry is not a sin. No, the sin blooms when anger is allowed to take root and overstay its usefulness or when that anger seduces us to take actions that should be beneath our best self. We are exhorted to not get angry quickly for "anger resteth in the bosom of fools" (Ecclesiastes 7:9, KJV).

If your anger doesn't take you to a place of peace and resolution, then it is a cancer cell waiting to embed itself in your soul and multiply destruction. I am often amazed at people who, in their workplace, have the skills to do an amazing job, be promoted, or even run the company, but who allow anger to poison their personality, potential, and power. In many cases, I've discovered that these individuals simply never learned how to use their anger in constructive ways. Unfortunately, we rarely learn how to resolve basic human conflict in our schools. So when certain people feel threatened or face conflict, they get vicious and vindictive. This isn't done because they are actively aggressive or tough; it occurs by default because they lack the skills to know how to let reason drive the car even when anger is the passenger.

These people create a toxic atmosphere in the office not because they want to but because they do not know how to move on. They confront well but then they have such acrimonious attitudes resulting from the confrontation that others no longer enjoy working with or for them. People perform so much more productively and creatively when the work environment is genuinely congenial.

It only takes one person who harbors hostility, disloyalty, or secret anger to infiltrate and poison an entire office. Yes, just one seething employee can end up giving an entire company a bad heart condition that decreases the functionality of the whole team. Every upper-level management person should be forced to take a course on conflict resolution and then to teach it to the other team members. We must equip ourselves first and then those around us with the tools we need to address and overcome the necessary confrontations and daily conflicts. It is harder to break rules that you have taught others about resolution; plus, it gives people recourse so they don't have to internalize and carry frustration, anger, and rage.

Here is a tip for those who are inclined to go too far and don't know how to get the equilibrium back in the office or home. I call it the two-for-one concept. For every confrontational moment you use to address what is bothering you, create at least two positive moments that affirm that the incident was the issue and not the person. Make sure that you are as articulate about other people's positive features as you were about what flustered you. If you correct the problem and lose the relationship, you didn't really gain— you lost.

Stress Test

We were not designed to harbor anger for long periods of time and internalizing it puts us in a constant state of stress. Like the blaring of an emergency siren, it is helpful in distress but annoying once the threat is past. Anger that overstays its welcome quickly becomes toxic and detrimental to the system it was trying to alert. Instead of signaling a fire or other calamity, the shrill alarm deafens us to the voice of reason. We no longer see clearly and lose sight of the "bigger picture."

Most child psychologists will tell you that children who harbor resentment and rage will display their malady in their class work. Their emotional development becomes stunted, and their internalized rage turns an otherwise well-developed child infantile. They have tantrums, sulk, mope, and lose some crucial years of healthy development because their anger has clogged their hearts and clouded their minds. While we don't like to admit it, the same is true for adults.

Let me provide you with a personal illustration. I know a pastor who has been part of our ministry for many years. He has been a part of our church's pastoral team the entire time I have been in Dallas and was also a part of my pastorate in West Virginia. So you might say I know him rather well. Not long ago, I happened to notice that he seemed unduly tired. He was still going about his tasks and duties as assigned and so I thought little of it. But I did encourage him to take a vacation when things slowed down a bit as he seemed like he could use one.

He said, "Oh, I'm fine, just a little tired." A month later he went to the doctor complaining of chest pains. They thought it was a reaction to some non-heart-related medications he was taking and ran a battery of tests to verify. However, his results all came back normal and the doctors were a little baffled. His electrocardiogram looked good, his vital signs seemed normal, and they saw nothing alarming. Just to be safe, his doctors decided that he should come back and do a stress test with dye just to make sure there were no hidden blockages. Fortunately, the pastor agreed and had the test done right away. If he hadn't, he might not have lived another day!

The test shocked all of us for it revealed that for quite some time he had been functioning with only 30 percent of his blood supply reaching his heart. He had undetected, unrealized blockages that were silently preventing most of the blood his heart needed to function from reaching that most vital organ. Needless to say, an emergency open-heart surgery ensued! Thankfully, he is recovering nicely and has started doing light duty in our church, as the surgery was successful.

I mention him because all of this time he wasn't getting full blood flow to his heart and didn't even know it. He didn't even know that the blockage existed much less what a toll it was taking on his heart. Like my pastor friend, you may still be standing, working, driving, parenting, or playing racquetball, but that doesn't mean that you are fine. You may only be operating on a small percentage of your full range of talents, capabilities, and skills, all because the silent assassin of anger has you in its sights.

Once his doctors replaced the clogged arteries with normal ones, this pastor found his energy and creativity skyrocketing. He never realized that he was working with only 30 percent of what he needed to function at top level. You can drive on the highway and gain speed with a stick shift stuck in low, but that doesn't mean you are at your best or that your engine won't suffer the consequences of being overtaxed.

So what is our spiritual stress test? How do we prevent our healthy anger from growing into a major blockage point? I believe that it's important to understand that even the most hideous of events in our lives have something to teach us, some purpose through which we can learn, be wiser, and grow stronger. First, I encourage you to gain perspective and see what you can draw from this experience that is positive and beneficial. Maybe it's a message to slow down, like a speeding ticket that unbeknownst to you may be saving your life from a deadly high-speed collision further down the road. Or perhaps it's a better appreciation of the many blessings and good gifts you have in your life. It could be a deeper understanding of yourself and your talents. Or maybe the newly acquired sensitivity can be a catalyst through which you can use your experiences to help others.

Once you have extracted all useable energy from the experience, you must attach the catheter and flush away the anger, bitterness, depression, self-loathing, or hatred of others. This is your responsibility to manage your emotions. Do not delegate the cleanup to someone else and excuse yourself from managing what you produced. If you don't, you will block the blessings and run the risk of missing the opportunity to move ahead unencumbered. If you don't use tools such as self-reflection, honest communication, counseling, and conflict management, then your anger will consume precious energy that could produce so much more.

Energy Crunch

The ratio of energy consumption to energy production continues to be a global problem of epic proportions, especially for us here in our country. It doesn't take a rocket scientist to realize that if we consume more energy, particularly from oil and gas reserves, than we produce, then we risk becoming vulnerably dependent on outside entities to assist with our energy needs. So today more than ever, we must realize the need to stop wasting our limited energy supply and instead develop an energy-efficient approach to our daily needs. To that end, we find a host of new products being developed and introduced every day with energy efficiency as their top priority.

Likewise we as humans only have a certain amount of time and energy to expend on the host of needs that we have. We, like our country, must make cuts where possible to preserve our energy for the most vital pursuits and avoid energy wastefulness. If you think of how much energy is expended through areas of anger, frustrations, and disappointments, you will quickly see that when people are not trustful of one another or when they are spending energy focused on retaliation or trying to survive in adverse circumstances, their energies could be reallocated toward more productive pursuits.

Consider how much energy you expend by sustaining an adversarial, war-mode approach on the job, in your marriage, or with those you encounter. You have to conserve your energy for its highest and best use. How much more productive, creative, and inno-vative would you be if you weren't directing such energies toward toxic relationships and defending yourself from people you have to work with or worship with?

As with my pastor's heart condition, your blockage may be preventing the majority of your energy from reaching the places that matter most. Like him, you can survive on a constricted flow of available resources. But you will never thrive, never explore the full capacity of your ability, and never enjoy the purpose for which God made you. When anger diverts your energy away from where it should be going, you fail to discover your highest and best use of your gifts.

When we experience blockages on our staff, we call it bottle-necking, the problem of slowing and choking the dissemination of much-needed information to the rest of the team. Often the in-formation is restricted in a person who has unresolved issues and doesn't communicate with this one or that one. Bottlenecking is often the result of someone's out-of-control control issues! Con-sequently, the company suffers from poor information or creative flow just like a heart functioning with less than needed blood. It can be expensive and detrimental to the welfare of the whole office.

If such a problem is identified, then a good manager will have to clear up the blockage by reprimanding or removing the indi-vidual so that the group can get the information that is needed to function at full capacity. This is yet one more reason why you can't afford to have angry or bitter people continue to come to work. It might be worth a stress test just to observe the flow of information and whether its path is obstructed in your workplace. It is there-fore in the best interest of the organization to clear the clutter, let go of that which would stop the greater good of people moving forward, and preserve the profit margins by eliminating the blockage. If that is true about business and bodies, it is also true about marriages and ministries.

This is often an emergency procedure. If it remains unrepaired, you have no way of knowing when the organization will have a proverbial heart attack and die from a completely avoidable malady. With my friend the pastor, the doctors took arteries from his leg that were unblocked and replaced the ones that were blocked in his heart and today he is healthy and functioning at full capacity.

It is clear with business. Unblocking the passages allows information, capital, and creative ideas to flow, resurge, and be disseminated. If you can't teach people within the organization to work only in a calm, polite, and professional way you are losing energy and creating a blockage in the soul of the department or company. You have no choice but to remove the blockage! The real test doesn't lie in the smile-while-I'm-looking type of office. The real test is more in the subtle innuendos that people do or say to cast shadows over others and use their influence to garner the support of previously neutral people, thereby spreading like cancer the poison to their associates about new or existing personnel. Now the cancer is spreading through the office, at the water cooler, during coffee breaks until the tumor surfaces in lost employees or lost opportunities. It sounds mean but I have learned as a CEO to be slow to hire and quick to fire. If you can't rehabilitate, you have to remove the blockage or the whole organization goes into cardiac arrest because you waited too long for the surgery!

I have often seen people take new employees and tell them whom to watch out for right from the beginning. They seem to want to ensure that the organization remains as constipated by their opinions and unforgiveness as possible. Remember, if you have been treated this way, not only do you need to forgive or be drawn into spreading the infection yourself, but you must also provide the antibiotic of rendering evil for good to stop the decay from spreading! We'll talk more about that in a subsequent chapter.

Heart Surgery

On a personal level, what arterial relocation have you done to refreshen the damaged areas in your life? Or what have you done to replace the damaged relationships, whether through reconciliation or, if that remains impossible, creating new ones to which you are now wiser and better suited to navigate?

Sometimes that may mean replacing people who disappointed or forsook you with healthier, less toxic relationships, thereby alleviating your extreme dependency on others' approval. You may have been the root cause of the blockage, asking people to be more to you than is possible and offended by their inability to fulfill voids too big for human hands to cover! It may mean replacing it with prayer. It could be that your decision to become involved with that person, confide in that person, graduate the relationship with that person is an expression of an inner need.

The need may be a natural one but the problem evolves when we try to resolve a legitimate need in an illegitimate way. It is where we seek solution that creates the plaque, the pain, the collapsing of relationships. Stop beating yourself up for being vulnerable to that need and start looking for healthier alternatives to past choices for the fulfillment of that need.

Of course, there are cases that create unforgiveness that are totally unsolicited by any need within the victim. Think of those angry from abuse or rape. They had no inner need to be raped, mugged, or maimed. But in the case of a "Bernie Madoff" situation where someone made off with your retirement, you can't spend the rest of your life being angry, you have to find a way to pick up the pieces, minimize the damages, and move forward with someone whose integrity can be traced, and honor can be restored.

I am encouraging you through prayer, counseling, or beating up a pillow to find a way to unblock your heart and move forward in your life. You don't want to waste your energy on that which was, while missing all that which is before you. Blessed are the pure in heart, for they shall see God. And live a joyful life to the fullest!

six

Write It Off

As we have discovered in the previous chapters, offenses are a part of life. Conflict can occur between people who truly love one another as well as those who barely know one another. Transgressions transpire between couples who have been married for fifty years as well as between strangers waiting at a bus stop. By now we are sure that life guarantees our attendance in this class of forgiveness whether we signed up for the course or not.

Sometimes the hardest lessons are the simplest. For example, as easy as it sounds to let go of the anger and resentment we hold toward our offender, it can be incredibly difficult to live out. In the process of trying to forgive and forget, we discover that sometimes a minor offense can do more damage than a major trauma. Depending on our reaction and how we choose to behave in light of a particular offense, a small slight can end up swelling into a cancerous growth if it remains unchecked.

While medication, chemotherapy, and radiation can often obliterate the cancer from a person's body, sometimes it is necessary to do invasive surgery and remove the malignant growth before proceeding with long-term treatment. Forgiveness often works the same way. Before we can proceed with healing and moving forward, we must separate ourselves from the power of an insidious preoccupation. We must let go of demanding that the wrong be righted, the loss be restored, or the offender be punished in the way that we deem appropriate.

Most of us grew up being taught a general set of societal rules, a value-based code of conduct, ethics, and principles that enable the world's inhabitants to interact with respect, fairness, and equity. However, if you're like me, it didn't take more than a few bullies on the school playground and a vindictive teacher to offer a very different portrait of the way the world operates. The reality is that life is not fair; sometimes the wicked prosper and the righteous suffer injustice. Yet we'd like to give most people the benefit of the doubt and assume that they hold a set of shared values in common with us. Unfortunately, this assumption or false expectation can wreak havoc with our ability to extend forgiveness.

In fact, from my experience, it seems the more highly principled you are, the more difficult it is to adjust to those people whose different principles (or lack thereof) become the catalyst for varying degrees of injury to your soul. To add insult to injury, some people seemingly have little to no values at all, which gives us real cause for great angst. When people do not share the same principles or disagree on how those principles should be upheld, then it can compound an already painful situation. Basically, injustice becomes salt in the wound we've suffered! Instead of our assailant being captured and punished for stabbing us in the back, his freedom and refusal to take responsibility enrage us all the more.

Common Decency

Some of us were Boy Scouts and Girl Scouts; others of us were altar boys in some ornate cathedral or candy stripers in a hospital ward. Some were principled by the faith tradition in which you were raised, and others have principles and values shaped by their parents' work ethic or cultural heritage. Regardless of the source and its means, the end goal remains the same: a sense of right and wrong and the moral courage to live within this awareness. Learning a healthy sense of right and wrong gave us an assurance that when conflicts arose we could appeal to a common level of decency and integrity. Surely we all have similar moral fiber and are guided by a similar GPS as to the determination of fair and unfair, right and wrong, good and evil. Isn't that right? No, it absolutely is not.

May I remind you that there are those who look as ordinary as an insurance adjuster who could break in a house and massacre the entire family one by one while eating a ham sandwich? We would like to think that such heartless, amoral people aren't real, that they are merely creations of fiction writers and Hollywood producers who need cardboard villains to entertain us. But art is really imitating life here, my friend.

Some would like to think that evil is always outwardly identifiable. Or that these people who commit such atrocities have some demonic scowl that separates them from the person we ride the subway with. We need this line of demarcation to hide from us the far more sinister truth that seemingly ordinary people can morph into inhuman monsters and do absolutely hideous things. This denial-based illusion seems to comfort us and in some way insulate us from the thin line between the rational and the irrational. The cold, gut-wrenching, nauseating truth is that most killers don't look like killers, no more than you can identify a thief by his mustache!

Understand, then, that if people's sense of decency can be so twisted that they can do the unimaginable without flinching, then they can easily lie to your boss so that they get that promotion instead of you. If a person could rob a bank and take multiple hostages and without any provocation destroy the life of ordinary people, if a young rapist could break into the house of someone's great-grandmother and brutally and fatally rape and kill this vulnerable woman, then surely you must realize that there are those among us every day who can swindle you out of your savings, distort truth for a superior position, write a check on a closed account, or avoid payment on a debt that they never intended to repay in the first place!

Most of us feel shocked and betrayed by those persons whose ethics and conduct violate our own sensibilities. It is disheartening and disgusting to find out that you have trusted someone on face value who betrayed that trust and seems to bear no sense of regret. When you start talking about forgiveness, you must be prepared to deal with a wide array of trauma incurred on the human soul.

Beyond Imagination

It was Father's Day, and I sent out a tweet encouraging people to find a way to love and embrace their father even if he wasn't the greatest dad they could have had. Pretty simple stuff, huh? Well, it was until I started to receive back responses that reflected the complications of families in crises. One lady reminded me in her tweeted response that not all of us who struggle with pain are lucky enough to deal with the garden variety of hurts, or what I like to call superficial wounds!

This lady tweeted back and said her father had murdered her mother and that he had been in prison, leaving her without either parent to draw some semblance of identity as a child and no sense of connectivity. In 140 spaces she had totally redefined family problems and taken it to the tenth power! Suddenly through the lens of her experience most other complaints and offenses seemed much more forgivable. It was clear that while hers may not be the normal testimonial, it was her reality. And her remarks prompted us to redefine whatever offense we may be struggling through.

Suddenly we thought that if she can forgive her father and wants to see him, those of us who had suffered lesser offenses and had hurdles to overcome could be strengthened to believe that forgiveness was indeed possible.

One of the best therapies for those who think their life is shattered is to climb out of the narcissistic cocoon that pain incubates in and see how many people all around you have so much worse to overcome and do so with grace and tenacity. When we are wronged and feel victimized we have a tendency to nurse our perspective, not seeing any other but our own, and become so preoccupied with our side of the story that we are seldom fair about the whole picture. But what is worse still is that we can eventually submerge so low that we feel justified to hate or harbor the lust for revenge. I told you about this lady to remind you that while some struggle to forgive a broken date or an embarrassing remark made at dinner, others wrestle with infidelity or improprieties, and still others struggle to forgive murder and rape. All forgiveness isn't created equal. But it all provokes similar questions!

What were they thinking about? Why didn't she just tell me the truth? How could he have overspent my credit card? I could understand it if it were this way or that way. In reality, most people who hurt us weren't really thinking about our needs at all. Most people are inherently self-enthroned egoists who aren't oriented to consider how their actions affect your well-being. Most people are so focused on their crises and need that they seem oblivious to what their actions have done to you. Their intentions aren't as much against you as they are "for" them.

The father left the family because he wasn't happy and didn't focus on what his actions would do to the child. Now the heart of the child hemorrhages emotionally, suffering from poor validation, not because of anything the child did but because the father was focused on helping himself and didn't really consider what his actions would do to his child! Most people are so selfish by nature that they are baffled (or even offended) by complaints about their behavior.

I have often asked myself, "How can you borrow money, not pay me back, and YOU end up offended? Could it be that your expectation of me is that I go quietly away without asking for what is rightfully mine?"

Savings and Loan

I remember many years ago getting a distressed call from an individual who desperately needed help with a car payment that had lapsed several months and the car was about to be repossessed. Given that he had children and was a rather highly visible person in the community, he was embarrassed and deeply worried about these economic crises.

It wasn't a good time for us financially, either, but when I heard of his challenge I told him I could get my hands on the money but would need it back as soon as possible. He agreed that he could meet the requirements and I went and got the money. I bet you already know what happened. Once he had secured the vehicle and anchored his circumstances with the money I loaned him, he never made any attempt to reimburse the amount or even to make the slightest payment toward it.

Initially he was very gracious but still not compliant with the agreement we had jointly made. As months passed and I had to struggle to replace the money he had borrowed my patience wore thin. I called, I wrote, I prayed, but still no money. Okay, I must tell you I got very angry and eventually rather hostile. What was interesting is that my discomfort wasn't met with repentance or payments or requests for patience but he became obstinate and irritated that I would ask for my money! I complained to a friend who is like a father to me. I began to rant about the unpaid money. But my friend finally told me: You are going to have to forgive the debt because you are never going to get your money back!

Now, this was very disturbing to me because I couldn't understand how you could act so pious in front of people or give special gifts to friends or even give charitable contributions and never get a dime toward the money I had in good faith spent to help my friend through a storm. What made matters worse is that I was trying to forgive someone who didn't even give me the dignity of a real apology. How can one forgive the unrepentant?

Never Said I'm Sorry

My mentor knew that every time I saw this individual my entire atmosphere was thrown off by his presence. When you are angry with someone or disappointed by something they did, their pres-

ence or cavalier attitude can leave you stuck on the road to forgiveness waiting on them to offer an apology before you get off
the highway of despair and move on. So when my mentor saw the
constant scowl on my face in the perpetrator's presence, he said to
me, "You might as well forgive the man, he is never going to pay
you back! If you remain bitter about this, you have given him control over your moods and are left with a response that is dictated
to you by his behavior." I didn't want to hear this sound advice
initially because forgiveness felt like he was getting off too easy!

When I look back on it, it is actually quite silly. How did my
not forgiving him hurt him? It didn't, which made me angrier.
How could he go out to dinner, laugh with friends, and move on
while I was still seething over what he had done? I finally had to
realize that my hurt and anger were attacking me but they weren't
hurting him. He was enjoying his life as if nothing had happened
while I was missing great moments because of the injury.

It is often hard enough to forgive when the person is repentant, but when they aren't even repentant and show no sign that
they will ever be, how can you stop the bleeding in your own life?
I am glad you asked. The truth of the matter is there are some
things that happen in life that you must forgive without the benefit of an apology, for your own emotional survival.

Now, before you totally reject this notion remember that people who aren't even alive to apologize have wronged some people.
If an apology is the only thing that will release the pain, you are
in an impossible dilemma. Some are angry with people who aren't
even in your circle anymore. You have removed the sting but the
swelling continues. Tormented on every turn, you feel helpless to
free yourself.

Think of the people who have had loved ones murdered and
go to a trial where the murderer doesn't even acknowledge that he

committed the crime much less apologize for it. Forgiving them doesn't exonerate them from guilt but it is done so that you aren't forever tied to the past.

Many years ago when I worked for a now defunct chemical plant I had a loan through my job for a credit union purchase I paid faithfully while employed. But once I was laid off and the company downsized, my wife and I went through an economic tailspin. As we spiraled down, running out of unemployment and still with no job, I finally got a short letter in the mail that said the credit union had written off the debt. One slash of a pen and they had removed it off the books and freed themselves from trying to collect the uncollectable.

Like that credit union loan, some legitimate debts are written off not because you didn't have a right to be paid but because the debtor lacks the ability to make right the wrong! In the same way the credit union didn't want to spend precious resources trying to collect the uncollectable, you and I must learn that in spite of your right to be vindicated or reimbursed, some people will not or cannot give you what is your due. The only way you can collect your energy and move forward is to simply write it off so that you can focus on what is ahead of you rather than forever being tied to what is behind you.

I encourage you to take back the power in your life even if the person cannot or will not right the wrong you have been done. Sometimes you must write the past off so that you are available for the future. You can't drive forward with your eyes affixed to the rearview mirror. In order to have your attention ready for the future you may glance back but cannot afford to become mesmerized or fixated on that which you have already passed by. Whatever is back there, write it off!

. . .

Let's understand a few things that will help you find the ability to release the past and move on.

1. Writing it off doesn't mean that you didn't gain anything from the experience. Often you have gained invaluable wisdom and discernment that will help you with future struggles.

2. Writing it off doesn't suggest that you weren't right about the abusive circumstances that led to the unforgiveness. It simply means you have too much ahead of you to expend more energy looking back.

3. Writing it off doesn't mean that you are weak. It takes a great deal of strength, hope, and faith to garner the courage to move beyond the breach.

4. Writing it off doesn't mean that you won't be compensated by some other opportunity ahead of you. Many times I really believe that God compensates us with divine favor to balance our lives beyond what was done to us by others.

5. Writing it off helps you to gain a glimpse into what God does for us with our own sin. We had a debt we couldn't pay. God received payment from an outside source (Jesus Christ) and wrote it off even though we ourselves never made recompense for our transgressions.

This is an extreme act of faith to believe that there is more ahead of you than there is behind you. But at the end of the day, you will miss your future swatting at your past. Simply write it off and keep moving!

Imagine the unforgiving person as being stuck in a stifling hot room in August in Phoenix. There is an air conditioner duct pointed at your head and yet you are sweating profusely. The room is filled with sweltering heat and you are about to go into a heatstroke! The reason you don't change the temperature is that you foolishly didn't build the house with a thermostat in the room. Often, the place where the heat is the most pervasive, there is no control system.

Similarly, when you allow someone else's reaction to determine your mood, you have built a room where you are helpless to control the climate. When you forgive them and move on you aren't acknowledging their innocence but your commitment to bring the thermostat back into your room and you leave them in the hands of their conscience and their God!

Of course you want to respond with grace to the repentant but the question begs an answer: What do you do when the persons who caused you the most pain have not and will not admit, acknowledge, or repent for their part in your pain? Simple answer, take the power back over your life and write it off. Demanding that they make things right or have the quality of character to apologize also leaves them controlling the thermostat to a room you have to live in.

Nowhere is there a more classic case of writing off a debt for an unapologetic individual than at the Cross, where the ones responsible for the Crucifixion didn't apologize and yet the first thing Christ did with the unrepentant was to ask the father to "forgive them for they know not what they do." How could he do this with blood running down his face and hands? How could he do that while the guilty further exacerbate the crises by gambling for his garments while he bleeds?

He does it because he has bigger issues to fight and he doesn't want to face a need to resurrect himself with any trace of bitterness draining his power. Frankly you also have to focus on resurrection and you can't get on with the business of resurrection if you are going to remain focused on the details of your personal crucifixion!

seven
Help Wanted

How many times have you been waiting on a document to print outside your cubicle when your coworker chastises you for jumping ahead of her? How many times have you been passed over for that promotion, knowing you're more qualified and experienced than the younger recipient, who just happens to be your boss's brother-in-law? How many times has another person on your shift erroneously blamed you for the malfunction on the production line? How many times has your supervisor taken credit for the innovative presentation that you envisioned, created, and executed from start to finish?

We've all experienced the harsh and often unexpected wounds that come from office skirmishes and workplace showdowns. From your first job as a teenager at the counter of a fast-food establishment to your current position at the conference table in the corporate boardroom, you don't have to be long on the job before you discover the petty politics, personnel hierarchy, and personal ambitions that rule the work world. With the exception of the marriage relationship, I would venture that no other environment produces more conflicts and requires more forgiveness than the place where we earn our living.

Researchers tell us that most of us spend over half our lives on the job—over half our lives! Although we change jobs more frequently nowadays, roughly every six to seven years, the ongoing sluggish economy has forced more people to work longer hours and to postpone retirement. Even people who once considered themselves "independently wealthy" have returned to the workforce as a result of market downturns and lower-yield investments.

Yes, we spend the majority of our waking hours at work—not with our family, not with those we love the most. No, they get what's left over from our forty to sixty hours consumed by the responsibilities of our employment. We give our spouse and kids a peck on the cheek, gobble down a portable meal, and dash out the door. They get what's left, usually not our best, and usually not what we want to give them. The tragedy of the twenty-first century may be that the people who mean the most to us get the least from us.

It's not only our time on the job that consumes our waking and working hours. Many of us who work in urban and suburban environments spend an exorbitant amount of time in our cars, stuck in traffic, driving to and from our workplace, trying to keep our blood pressure from rising when the pickup truck cuts us off. Even our commute to the office requires forgiveness when you think about it! When I drive on the interstate, I don't want people to know I'm a pastor for fear they will notice the murderous rage in my eyes directed toward the sweet grandmother driving ten miles below the speed limit in the passing lane. If you're one of those drivers who takes her sweet time no matter where you're going, then please forgive me!

When there is internal fighting in the office, then the turmoil will lead to mediocrity and eventually destruction. Like the Roman Empire imploding from within, a workplace defined by strife and competition will eventually be defined by defeat. Where there is no cohesion, no compromise, and no collaboration, there will be collapse. This is not spiritual mumbo jumbo. Your bottom line, your income, your productivity and profitability are directly affected by the baggage strapped to your shoulders, regardless of your ability to see it or your willingness to acknowledge it.

Isn't it time to go to work and let it go?

Who's the Boss?

For the vast majority of people, the pressure to perform is the strongest in the workplace. We are evaluated by what we do, by our ability to achieve the desired results, by how well we can satisfy customers and placate coworkers. As one CEO once told me, "Many deficits in an employee's personality are overlooked if they make their bottom line." While this mind-set poses problems of its own, it remains one of the harsh realities of the corporate world. At home we are loved for who we are; at work we are assessed by what we do.

This kind of performance pressure often requires us to set aside our emotions and focus on desired outcomes, profitability, and solutions to the barriers inhibiting productivity. We can't wait until we feel inspired to put together the big presentation. We can't turn down an assignment just because our supervisor forgot to say "please" when she asked us. And we can't hold grudges, not for very long at least, because when we do, we stifle not only our own productivity but eventually the success of the organization as well.

Perhaps no one causes and receives more wounds in the work-place than those in charge. By virtue of holding authority over other employees, they wield their sense of responsibility and power, causing a wide range of offenses. Many supervisors discover that those they oversee are biased against them before they have ever had any direct interaction with them. When management positions are filled from outside of the company, new hires may be resented for not knowing the already established institutional systems. Leadership positions filled from within may produce supervisors who already have a history and are perceived by those around them as only qualified for the accounting or marketing or whatever department from which they came.

Leaders who find themselves embroiled in ongoing office tensions often discover that the issue has nothing to do with them or their leadership style. By virtue of their position, they become the target for all kinds of issues that their employees simply do not know how to leave outside the office door. It may be authority issues and feelings of resentment, rebellion, and retaliation. It may involve projecting issues that stem from the employee's relationship with their father or mother. It may be a desperate desire for affirmation that can only be filled by personal relationships, not professional ones.

Releasing our boss, our manager, our team leader from the grudges that we harbor is easier said than done. One of the beautiful aspects of working collaboratively is the variety of colorful personalities and brilliant skill sets that converge to create and sell new products, promote and market those products with innovative resources, and lead the organization at the right pace for consistent, healthy growth. We could model forgiveness even as we extend it to those we serve when mistakes are made, whether the offense be an unnecessarily harsh word on the conference call or a mistake in addition on the expense report.

In an ideal world, those who lead and supervise us would be wiser, more experienced, and more mature than those under their supervision. Our bosses would be compassionate and understanding, fair and firm, inspiring and intuitively gifted at directing others in a way that motivates them to their peak performance. However, again, one does not have to work at a job for long to witness the weaknesses, inconsistencies, and even incompetency of those who are often in charge. In many cases, we correctly perceive that we are better equipped to make the decisions that are made for us in the workplace, and often this is a source of our greatest frustration.

One of the regrettable practices within corporate America is that the talented practitioners inevitably rise into management. I know dozens of gifted doctors, scientists, carpenters, architects, and teachers who no longer come in contact with a stethoscope, a test tube, a hammer, protractor, or chalkboard! Their giftedness leads to praise and recognition, which then elevates their superiors' awareness of their abilities. Then the assumption is made that because they are gifted at what they do that they will be equally talented at leading others in the field.

Unfortunately, this is often not true and only leads to resentful frustration on the part of the promoted practitioner and confused disappointment on the part of those who promoted them, not to mention the frustrations of the employees sandwiched in between. Sometimes the best leaders may have had little to no experience with the particular products in the field in which they lead. Sometimes the most astute CEOs are those who know how to motivate, inspire, and empower those around them, not the ones who create, build, and sell the company's products.

Similarly, the best supervisors know how to build trust, inspire confidence, and delegate responsibility to those whom they choose to serve directly under them. This has certainly been the model to which I have aspired over the course of over three decades, not only as a pastor and ministry leader, but as an entrepreneur in a variety of endeavors. People will sometimes ask me how I am able to do all that I do, how I manage to go from a women's conference to a film production meeting to a radio interview all in the same day (sometimes before lunch!).

My response is that I take great care and deliberation in selecting those who will be the guardians to the doorways of my various enterprises. When I hire someone or appoint someone into a position of authority and responsibility, I'm already 99 percent certain that I can trust them with the job and therefore have no trouble delegating quickly.

I believe that we can prevent a vast number of the altercations and offenses that occur in the workplace simply by hiring that right person for the right job. Certainly, there are some positions in which a person can be allowed to grow into their responsibilities. But these are usually called entry-level positions, not upper management. We must groom talent from within our organizations but also allow ample time for maturity and social development to occur.

When the prophet Samuel was led by God to anoint David as king of Israel, the shepherd boy did not immediately assume the throne and begin making crucial decisions of national importance. In fact, he continued on as a shepherd and a soldier before he eventually took his place on the throne. He became seasoned by his life experiences that kept him grounded and in touch with the everyday needs of those whom he was chosen to serve. He never forgot what it was like to face a giant named Goliath and overcome insurmountable odds to defeat a foe perceived to be unconquerable.

If you are harboring grudges against your boss or supervisor, I encourage you to write him or her a letter in which you attempt to be as honest as possible. Whether or not you send your letter is up to you, but I have found that the simple act of articulating my grievances against someone can help me look at them and my perception of the offense more objectively. In some cases, you will read over your letter and realize that you're projecting a problem where none exists. In others, you'll realize that your productivity will not increase unless you deal honestly with your supervisor. The temptation will be strong to talk behind his or her back, to complain, grumble, and even gossip because of the offense that festers within you. You must resist this common quagmire of corporate unforgiveness by first speaking with the person who has offended you, not with everyone else.

In many cases, your boss or coworker may not even be aware that they offended you and that you're upset. And sometimes, both your expectations and theirs need clarification in order for you to understand each other, discern what is coming between you, and find a way to forgive and forge onward. Otherwise, you may end up using your boss as a bull's-eye for your own emotional baggage without even realizing it.

Great Expectations

A close friend, I'll call him Dylan, recently told me about a messy situation in which he found himself confronted with difficult decisions to make regarding the marketing team he led for a large Fortune 500 company. His role required him to travel frequently, often overseas, which meant that he was not always present in the office for regular meetings and one-on-one encounters with his team members. He liked his team members but had inherited all of them from his predecessor except for a junior associate whom he had recently hired.

After returning from five days of international strategy meetings in London, my friend returned to the office and discovered that the weekly team meeting that he had canceled while he was away occurred without him. The associate he had hired himself, Leslie, told him, albeit a bit reluctantly, that it was basically a gripe session about Dylan's many flaws according to the veterans who had been in the company longer. Two team members in particular, a woman named Yvonne who had been there twenty years, and Eric, a late twentysomething who had been there since he had interned while in college, led the charge.

Long story short, my friend Dylan confronted each team member and got very different reactions, in fact the opposite of what he expected. Apparently his relationship with Yvonne had always been prickly and so he expected denial and resistance. However, when he confronted her, she burst into tears and confessed that she had applied for the job he now had and really had nothing against him other than being the daily reminder that she, once again, had not advanced. She asked for forgiveness, which he granted, and then he promised to review her career goals and promotional advancement strategy the following week.

Eric, on the other hand, was someone with whom Dylan had always enjoyed a productive, communicative relationship. Eric had directly asked Dylan to mentor him and seemed to consult his boss on virtually every decision. When Dylan confronted Eric, expecting an apology after his talk with Yvonne had gone so well, he watched his young associate turn from a doting acolyte into a Machiavellian manipulator before his very eyes. Eric snarled that he was smarter than Dylan and that it was only a matter of time before he pushed him out the door and took his job. Eric regretted being exposed but refused to apologize for anything he had said at the impromptu meeting when Dylan was absent.

Dylan said nothing for several moments, but then stood and asked Eric to wait there until he returned in a moment. When he reentered the room, he was accompanied by the human resources director. With absolutely no glee whatsoever, Dylan fired Eric on the spot and the HR supervisor accompanied him out of the building. Eric was stunned and began protesting, but it was too late. His lack of respect would not be tolerated by his boss or by the organization.

I tell you this story for two reasons. First, you must never assume that you know how a confrontation will go in the workplace. Based on prior history and the existing relationship, my friend erroneously assumed how his conversations with his two rebellious team members would go. However, each not only responded differently but revealed deeper issues that needed to be addressed. Yvonne needed to own her disappointment, let go of her resentment at the organization, and give her boss a chance to do things his way, not hers. Eric, on the other hand, had managed to hide his ruthless ambition beneath a veneer of benign loyalty.

Five for Fighting

Which leads to my second point: Never be afraid to enter into a confrontation. So often, we want everyone to like us and think we're a nice person. Christians often compound this by adding a layer of self-righteous religiosity to the mix. They feel like it would be a sin to criticize a team member, even constructively, and thus smile and nod and accept less than desirable outcomes.

Psychologists tell us that there are five basic strategies for facing conflict: **1. avoiding; 2. commanding; 3. accommodating; 4. compromising;** and **5. collaborating.**

Sometimes it's okay to avoid conflict or postpone a confrontation. Some altercations are unnecessary to dissect and discuss and will dissolve on their own without your involvement. As the old saying goes, "You have to pick your battles." In other words, you must make sure that the confrontation is worth the energy and effort. If you know a coworker is leaving your department in two weeks, then it may not be the most effective investment to plan a meeting to discuss her failure to turn in her quarterly goals.

Commanding, or forcing your viewpoint in the midst of conflict, may sound like an unpleasant, authoritarian style of resolving problems, but sometimes, particularly in times of crisis, it may be necessary for someone to make a crucial decision even if it's unpopular. When a rival company is attempting a hostile takeover, there may not be time to hold a board meeting, follow scheduled protocol, and get the input of all stakeholders. Similarly, accommodating may sound positive but could be detrimental if you are giving up items that you need to maintain. On the other hand, if you can accommodate someone's request in a way that doesn't cost you and your department very much, then by all means it's worth the goodwill engendered to acquiesce.

Compromise is perhaps the most useful tool when dealing with conflict and making a confrontation. This strategy allows for both parties to receive part of the solution they requested, yet no one gets everything they wanted. As basic as it may sound, the key to effective compromise is making sure you are comfortable with the give-and-take inherent in the exchange. The trade-off must be equitable and resolve the problem in a way that allows forward progress to be made by both individuals. I can't tell you how many individuals have come to me complaining about a confrontation with a coworker in which they compromised even while their blood was boiling under their starched shirts and silk blouses.

The fifth style of handling confrontation, collaborating, allows for both parties to get everything they wanted in the situation. In actuality, many conflicts could be resolved with simple collaboration; however, this often requires someone to apologize, ask for forgiveness, or take responsibility, all of which may sound good in Sunday school but are hard to practice at your Monday-morning staff meeting.

Most people naturally gravitate toward one style based on their personality and past conditioning. However, no one style should be considered better than another; each one is beneficial in its own way and could be considered the best option depending on contextual circumstances. All five of these styles of handling confrontation are effective in the right situation. The key is to know your default style, the response you naturally gravitate toward perhaps without even realizing it. It's not that your default style is wrong or ineffective, only that it's limited. When you are aware of your tendencies to rely on it, you can then pause and consider the other four possible strategies. You want to carry all five with you in your tool belt. Sometimes you need a hammer and other times a screwdriver or pliers.

Peer Pressure

In addition to the conflicts and offenses that occur with our bosses and supervisors, we must look from side to side at those with whom we work shoulder to shoulder on a daily basis. Too often, we perceive our coworkers as our enemies, not potential allies. We have trained our mind to doubt the good intentions of anyone at face value and assume that our peers are adversaries out to intimidate, undermine, and overturn everything we do.

I have talked to so many people who find themselves promoted in their jobs and then seem stunned at what's required to lead their team. As one new supervisor told me, "I had no idea that people could be so, so . . . *needy!*" Yes, the vast majority of people bring their personal needs into the workplace. They simply cannot contain it. Consequently, they can't be effective on teams. They cannot be managed. And they can't fulfill their full potential.

There's nothing focused around the goal or common objectives with coworkers. Instead we create chaos. People who work together find their personal lives spilling over the tops of cubicles and into production lines, out of boardrooms and into golf courses and country clubs. Their prejudices, biases, and opinions become the social currency they use to try and develop the relationships necessary to do business.

However, what begins as a polite conversation in the break room quickly turns into voyeuristic details of their marriage, counseling sessions about their kids, and personal therapy about their childhood. The office refrain has become "TMI," too much information. And it's not only the personal issues and unwanted minutiae of their lives that bombard our coworkers. It's too much competition, frustration, and exasperation. The work environment has become toxic and it has nothing to do with the requirements of the job itself and everything to do with the personal issues eclipsing everyone's time, focus, energy, and attention.

We must learn to keep the main thing, the main thing. If we don't, then the main thing will slip through our fingers and we will become distracted by myriad urgent demands and current crises that have nothing to do with becoming more productive or effective in our job responsibilities.

Talent is important, but only focusing on the talent of a few instead of the focused talent of the team will undermine the organization's success. There must be delegating, regulating, and accountability. We must learn to keep altercations in the locker room and not on the playing field. Just because you used to date my old girlfriend should not prevent you or me from scoring a touchdown in the game. We must be determined to keep the main thing, the main thing.

So many people are afraid of not getting the credit they deserve. But here's the thing: Excellence cannot be hidden. You don't have to tell someone you're an excellent salesman; simply make your pitch and show them. If you have to tell someone that you're such an amazing preacher, then I wonder how good you really are. The people who are truly excellent do not have to tell anyone because their talent speaks for itself. If you are doing your best and striving for excellence, then there is nothing to worry about. No one can steal your credit or exceptional performance. It speaks for itself.

No Trespassing

In our examination of the Lord's Prayer, you'll recall the request that we make to God: "Forgive us our trespasses as we forgive those who trespass against us." Sometimes this is translated as "Forgive us our debts," but the word "trespasses" seems perfectly suited for the workplace.

Whether in the lines of our job description or the size of our desk and location of our office, we are ever mindful of encroachment and inequity in our place of employment. In the workplace, too often we become rigid about boundaries and want to keep things in straight-line configurations. But success does not remain contained within flow charts and reporting structures. As in traffic, some will veer over into our lanes, and we will find ourselves drifting into the lanes of others. Our workplace is a high-occupancy vehicle lane! There are lots of comings and goings, darting in and out of one another's lanes.

Great minds tend to trespass because they think in circles not in lines. In the workplace, from time to time it's necessary to cross lines and multitask. When individuals start saying, "That's not my job!" then it's clear that no job is truly being done well. The marketer will be required to sell, the salesman will be required to design, the researcher will be required to manage in a healthy, growing, successful organization. And if we are not helping one another grow across disciplines in order to function more effectively as a team, then we will never be unified in our mission.

When my wife was in college, she joined a sorority, and one of the requirements for her and her sister pledges was rather unique. They were required to recite the entire Greek alphabet while passing a lit match round-robin among them. When I asked her about it recently, she laughed and said, "Woe to the sister who received the match and didn't immediately know her letter!" But what my wife and her new sisters learned is that when one of their pledge class members stumbled, they all failed.

"We were not only responsible for making sure that we knew the Greek alphabet. We were responsible for making sure all of our sisters knew the Greek alphabet as well," she told me. Like many of the military exercises that new recruits endure at boot camp, this team-building discipline bonded members together in a way that made it clear that it was not every person for themselves, but that the whole team was defined by its weakest link. No one was allowed to fail because that meant the team would fail.

Trespasses will naturally occur and so you must become accustomed to both giving and receiving forgiveness. The benefits are manifold. Practicing forgiveness allows you to be fulfilled by your job. You will never be satisfied in your job until you learn to forgive those with whom you work. Practicing forgiveness in the workplace increases your opportunities for promotion and advancement within the organization. You will not be promoted and advance in your career without grace and mercy. Finally, practicing forgiveness equips you to be a leader when opportunities present themselves. You will not be an effective leader or productive innovator unless you learn the art of forgiveness.

eight

Trust Doesn't Come Easy

After we have identified an offense and have accepted the offender's apology, we often find ourselves in a unique position to rebuild something that we watched crumble before our very eyes. It's like looking at a building that appears sound and solid through and through, well built and well supported, and then suddenly finding ourselves gawking as it collapses from within. Like the once-impenetrable Twin Towers falling on 9/11, we rarely see terrorists' intentions unfold until it's too late.

Many relationships deteriorate in the same way once trust has been breached. You suddenly realize that what you thought you had was not as substantial as it appeared. Now you have an empty building site and tricky questions arise, "Do I dare rebuild another structure on the same site? If so, what will prevent this building from collapsing like the last one?" In other words, how do you rebuild that most precious construction material of trust?

Understand that trust is a valuable commodity that cannot be purchased with credit. In its purest form it cannot be based on the benefit of the doubt. Trust is far more expensive and far more exotic than what can be attained through happenstance. Trust is based on probable behavior. Trust means being able to predict what other people will do and what situations will occur.

If we can surround ourselves with people we trust, then we can create a safe present and an even better future. Simply stated, trust is built on the foundation of our past experiences with an individual or corporation. It has little to do with loving or liking an individual or entity. It has everything to do with the comfort level whereby you sink your full weight into that probable behavior.

Have a Seat

Think about trust this way. When we sit in a chair we don't try to trust or encourage ourselves to relax. We place the weight of our body into the arms of the furniture because we have reason to expect it to hold us up. If that expectation hasn't been fulfilled by past experiences, then we warily approach the piece of furniture wondering if it has been repaired in such a way to now bear our weight. We are justified in having a natural reaction to those past experiences that cause us to lose trust and approach the chair with caution.

Imagine that you sat down at the dining room table and the chair gave way to the weight of your body. Very few if any of us would return to that chair and place our full weight on it again without some degree of caution. If we were to try to sit in the chair again, our minds would graciously remind us of what happened the last time and our common sense would make us proceed with caution. After all, who wants to fall and bust their caboose a second time?

The onus of restoring trust lies in large part on the offender who let us down. Such trust can only be restored when a history is cataloged of continual and consistent unwavering behavior that supports us more substantially than our past encounters. Until the vast majority of recent data replaces the pattern and proclivity for disappointment, we are not likely to trust again. In other words, we need to inspect the new building materials if we are truly going to believe the new structure to be stronger than its predecessor.

You can't make yourself trust what you don't trust. No more than you can make yourself love a person you don't love. Trust when damaged can be rebuilt, but the trust builder has to be willing to punch the clock and do the time to rebuild what was lost in the fall. The reason the victim cannot bear the brunt of responsibility to trust again emerges when we consider that they were already willing to trust in the past and got burned for it. Trust can only be formed from the basis of experiences we have had. In order to rebuild the trust, the one who destroyed the relationship's structure must now create an atmosphere in which what they say and what they do align. Otherwise, the entire building site may be destroyed if the offender once again betrays you.

Fool Me Once

Most psychologists would agree that the best predictor of future behavior is past experience. If you met William, who had been married five times and all past wives were mysteriously murdered, it would be wise to keep your eyes wide open when William is around! If Joe molested his daughter, his niece, and his cousin, then please forgive me if I don't ask him to babysit for me! Do you really have to think about whether to ask your bank-robber neighbor who's just been paroled to make a deposit for you?

The bad news is trust takes time to rebuild. The good news is with the proper investment and a willingness to endure copious inspection while rebuilding, trust can and will be restored given time to reestablish itself. Most people who have violated a trust have a tendency to minimize how long it takes to rebuild it. They are anxious to rebuild it quickly and become impatient if the other party takes longer than they think they should. These offenders don't seem to realize that's it's easier to repair the broken chair than it is to regain the confidence of the man who broke his hip bone from the last time the chair gave way.

While it is without a doubt the burden of the trust breaker to rebuild that trust, he or she isn't the only one who has work to do. The one who has been victimized by the loss of trust has a responsibility to demonstrate that they are willing to rebuild on the same site. The victim must be willing to allow that trust process to be rebuilt. Some people, no matter how much you do and how you do it, will not allow you to forget what you did in the past. It's like losing a house to a soft foundation and then trying to rebuild it on quicksand. It's a futile endeavor—and restoration of trust is impossible, unless both parties commit to the rebuilding process.

So understand that yes, the person who lost trust has to work to be open to trusting again. However, they must come to such a willingness by their own decision. They cannot repair the loss of trust by coercion or guilt placed on them to hurry to heal. The person who has violated the trust must be prepared to walk down the long road to healing. Perhaps the long process is what makes the return of trust valuable and therefore not desecrated easily. If trust comes cheap, it isn't valuable and will likely reinjure itself again.

Much like the rebuilding of the levees after Hurricane Katrina, when it rains there is a tendency for the citizens of New Orleans to check the docks and the flood walls. It will likely take time for another hurricane to strike and the city's inhabitants not be at least somewhat apprehensive considering what happened last time.

The reflection on what happened, whether expressed outwardly or not, is a real aftereffect of the violation. It may take several storms for the homeowner who lives by the levee not to run to the window and look out nervously and inquisitively. I am sure most of us would not be surprised by such a reaction. However, many times we expect those who had to swim through our last indiscretion, disloyalty, or inconsistency to immediately relinquish all reservation. That simply isn't likely.

What would it take for you to hire Sally back if the last two times she stole out of the cash register? What would it take for you to trust James to lock the back door when he left it open several times before? It would take him repeatedly rectifying his past neglect by maintaining a consistency of performance—locking the door—that rebuilds trust. And he should not be offended because you're prone to run back and check to see if the back door is locked! He knows that he has created this problem by the experiences you had with him, and if he sincerely wants to regain your confidence, then he has to be willing to let you check up on him until such time as you can comfortably rest in full restoration of his renewed responsibility.

Closed for Business

One of my uncles used to say something that often confused me as a child, a remark he would make usually after renewing acquaintance at a family reunion with some long-lost cousin who owed him money! My uncle would say, "I love them—they're family. I just can't do business with them." It wasn't until I was older and wiser (and had a few cousins of my own who owed me) that I understood what he meant. You can love someone without giving them everything they ask for. In fact, when we try to maintain someone's love by giving in to their demands, we often kill the relationship.

Real love has nothing to do with trust. Neither does forgiveness. It is highly possible to love someone you do not trust. It is also highly feasible to forgive someone and still not trust them. We are never commanded in Scripture to trust someone. I'm convinced the reason God doesn't command us to trust others is because trust is not something we can establish on our own. Trust cannot be restored by only one person in the relationship. So it would be unfair to command us to do something that has so much to do with someone else's behavior!

While we aren't commanded to trust, we are commanded in Scripture to forgive. Forgiveness is something within your power to rebuild, even alone if necessary! But trust needs a partner or it can't come to the prom!

How long does it take to rebuild the trust? This is a great question for which there is no simple answer. It leads to other questions. How deep was the wound? How fast does the victim take to heal? How patient are you to allow them to vent, cry, complain, go through mood swings, and all else to regain their trust? While the violation or betrayal may have lasted only seconds, it can take years to restore all that collapsed in those brief few moments.

Construction Crew

Trust restoration is a joint effort. There must be other qualities in the process if the new construction is to withstand the test of time. Just as rebuilding a home lost to a hurricane or tornado requires the collaborative effort of a construction team—carpenters, electricians, plumbers, to name a few—so must we employ additional workers to produce our new building. Trust can be rebuilt when the following additional workers are brought to the site and join the construction crew.

1. **Honesty** lays a new foundation. You can't rebuild trust if you can't admit that trust has been violated.

2. **Understanding** why the offender betrayed you is often a necessary part of rebuilding trust. What was the offender's motive or gain for the offense? If you can't discuss why it happened, trust will remain uncomfortable.

3. **Consistency** provides the structure for renovating trust. There needs to be a continual practice of conduct to keep moving forward. It's difficult to expect a scab to form and the skin to heal fully over a wound that you keep reinjuring. No, the wound must have constant care and ongoing protection if the body is to heal completely. A constant, steady diet of care helps trust to heal more rapidly.

4. **Communication,** open and ongoing, allows trust to bloom again in depleted soil. Trust needs to talk. If trust can't discuss, it can't rebuild. Some of the hardest things to heal are the things we hide and the secrets we keep. They are hard to heal because trust needs to clear the air. You can't push the mute button and expect trust to incubate in the silence of suppressed expression.

Understand that trust needs time to heal but forgiveness is a decision. It is an act of one's will. It is a choice you make of your own accord. The restoration of trust doesn't always respond in all people at the same time. Some people have the capacity to throw off pain more readily than others. For many people, the particular incident that caused us to lose trust is not the only experience with such pain.

So when we are looking at the reinjury of a past wound, often the process takes longer as the person senses a pattern in their own life that makes them question their own judgment. It isn't just that the distruster has lost confidence in the one who hurt them. What often goes unsaid is that more times than not, the victim has lost confidence in their own ability to discern what is true. This is often the most difficult aspect of the process.

Have you ever doubted your own judgment? You meet someone and have a certain first impression. After you get to know them and trust them, they betray you. If you can relate, then you understand the courtroom-style badgering that occurs in the trial taking place in your own head. You accuse and indict yourself for being a fool simply because you didn't see it coming or you ignored what you saw in your first impression.

Consequently, any conversation that you have with others about trusting becomes nothing compared to the Ping-Pong match you replay in your mind. No one knows but the injured how deeply their distrust extends. A hurtful situation can leave you isolated with self-flagellating words swarming like bees to honey. So then rebuilding isn't just about regaining the trust within a relationship or from a coworker. When emotional deposits have been rewarded with bankruptcy, depression ensues along with a fear of investing in anyone else ever again. When we lose faith in our ability to discern and choose for ourselves, then we withdraw from living our lives to the fullest. We conclude that other people cannot be trusted and apparently nor can we trust our own judgment of them!

A Time to Heal

All of us have watched the aftermath and devastation of a community that has been ravaged by an unexpected tornado. With the roof ripped from a house like a massive can opener had peeled it back, the once-precious personal items of a family are now strewn through the community for miles. Cars hang from split trees, tractors sit on top of barns, and massive debris makes the scene indistinguishable from a dump site for the city trash. In the face of such gnawing helplessness and despair, the majority of the destruction zone's inhabitants will return and build again.

In spite of all the emotional, physical, and economic loss, in spite of the likelihood that it will take years to recover from the devastation before them, they still teach us that what really matters remains intact. The life of their loved ones, a place to come home to, a sense of family, community, and connection to those around them. Many of them recognize how blessed they are to survive the tornado. With a stern look of defiance and gratitude they say, "We can rebuild."

If your relationship is brought down to ground level zero and trust has been battered by the winds of life, if your coworker has exploited you and now you cry all the way to work on a job that you love in a situation that you despise, consider what you have left rather than what was destroyed. *No one rebuilds on what they lost.* Rebuilding begins when you appreciate what you have left.

For some marriages shattered by humiliation and public or private disgrace, all they have left is love. Sure it may be cracked by distrust, and the frame has been twisted by the harsh winds of unsuspected secrets. But the core of what matters, the portrait beneath the glass and within the frame, yet remains. Sometimes you don't know what matters until you have lost all else. Many couples, finally free of secrets and forced by the storm to be totally honest, discover that rebuilding, though tedious and stressful, is yet possible.

They discover that what really matters most to them is still intact. Ironically enough, it took the destruction of the storm to remove the other layers and reveal what exists beneath it all. Some of them are back to being honest with each other in a way they have not been for years. Though they have lost a lot, they have found something in the debris and they decide to rebuild the trust!

I have seen staff members rebound from a situation so devastating that all around them view them with doubt and distrust. Most quit or are fired but some strap on their boots and wade into the standing waters of suspicion and begin, case by case, to redefine themselves. They work hard and ultimately win the respect of all because they made the difficult choice to stay and rebuild.

Above the Offense

Many years ago one of my children stole some money from me. I had left my wallet in my closet with several hundred dollars in it. While it might sound careless, most of us like to believe that our possessions are safe and protected within the confines of our own homes. It wasn't an incredible amount of money, but that wasn't the point. And this wasn't a small child but one old enough to know better.

To be quite frank, I felt like I'd been slapped in the face. I suppose my hurt must have been obvious. I didn't care about the money, but the defiant disregard for all else but my child's need was painful to see. I put up a strong front of anger and discipline. But beneath it all I was simply hurt that my own child could violate my trust and rob me. I went on and on to myself about not being able to leave anything lying around in my own house, I pined about all I had done for them and how I would have given it to the child anyway had they asked. And then day by day, I survived like we all do when we've been hurt and found a way to love above the offense.

Later I would grow as a father and begin to understand that though my child was wrong, so was I. My worldview and perceptions were unrealistic. It's amazing how self-righteous you can get when you are the victim! I actually forgot something similar that I had done when growing up. Isn't it amazing how we have a tendency to deny people the grace that we ourselves have needed at some point in our lives?

Besides, after raising five children, I now understand that adolescence is supposed to be tumultuous! I realize that most teenagers can't help being selfish as they are trying feverishly to cross the bridge from being "your child" to becoming "their own person." It's a big adjustment for the parent and the child as you embark on the task of redefining the terms of your relationship. Generally, parents don't like letting go and young people see them as controlling instead of loving. No matter how kind and good the child may be, they have never had to cross such a bridge to adulthood and there are no rules to guide them. They are generally so confused, being not quite a woman but no longer a little girl. They struggle with "mannish" ways and boyish values. Often they are so consumed with getting across that bridge that they generally do some damage along the way. If you guide them and don't become such an idealist that you hold on to your rules at the expense of losing the child, you meet up again on the other side of the storm.

Several months went by and things had pretty much normalized when one day out of the blue my child had this emotional outburst. With a face flooded by tears he said, "Daddy, I don't know how to fix it!" I thought, "Fix what?" Whatever was going on at the moment had nothing at all to do with this old issue that was to me over and done with. My pain had receded but what I didn't know is that my child had been rattled by guilt and shame far beyond what I could've ever imagined.

He later would tell me how he loathed himself for disappointing me. That he suffered night after night crying himself to sleep. Sometimes people seem like they aren't that remorseful outwardly, but that doesn't mean that they don't cry in the night. Somehow knowing that I wasn't just angry but hurt had crushed my child more than it had me.

You see, when people sincerely love you, they also hate disappointing you. If you watch life closely, read the paper, or follow the news, you will eventually observe that just because someone can throw a ball doesn't mean that they know how to be a husband. Or just because someone can make great speeches doesn't mean that they manage money well. All of us have areas in which we lack abilities, skills, or experience. Often those whose talents seem the most impressive carry the most shame about their deficiencies.

People who are strong in one area are usually weak in another. All of my children are very gifted and talented; each one has areas that they excel in. Though my son could have been weak in one area or made a foolish, selfish, and painful choice, it doesn't mean he doesn't have much to offer. There is a difference between weakness and wickedness. I am sure if you are a good parent you can relate to what I am saying. But what baffles me is how compassionate we can be for our own children and not realize that the lady who wronged us or the guy who didn't give us credit for the work everyone knows we did is not unforgivable! Please remember that they are somebody's child, too. Maybe you can stick to your values without destroying the individual.

Though tested by many other storms along the way, my relationship with my children never went through that test again. At the end of the day, the offense wasn't as important to me as my child, and ultimately I had to allow my prodigal son a way back home. Your openness to rebuilding trust is an important test of your own character. If we deny others mercy, then by our own design we maintain that redemption is not possible for the guilty!

Yes, trust takes time, just like rebuilding a house after a storm takes time. But just because something is difficult doesn't mean it isn't worth it. Sometimes the real treasure comes in the building process. Open communication ensues, weaknesses are exposed, and intimacy begins to build. The relationship that was once shattered—the boss you used to almost loathe, the very friend you thought would never help you—may be the relationship that long-term gives you the greatest joy. What all of us really want is someone who could see our most hideous frailties and love us anyway. But the tragic irony is that we want something from people that we often do not give ourselves. We must remember our Lord's Prayer: "Forgive us our trespasses as we forgive those who trespass against us."

If you have been knocked down to the foundation and all you have left is shattered love, then maybe it's time to rebuild. Love and kindness often take a real beating in the process of any socialization with another flawed individual. But you will never regret taking the high road. Forgiveness is a choice. Once you decide to extend it, it will travel first-class. I have learned that forgiveness may take a jet but trust travels on the bus, sees all the sites, and explores its surroundings. Trust may arrive later than love or long after forgiveness, but it is far richer from the journey!

nine
Recovery Rate

While the whole world watched with anticipation of holding someone other than the icon they lost responsible, Michael Jackson's doctor, cardiologist Conrad Murray, was recently found guilty of manslaughter in the untimely death of his most famous patient. Amid the dramatic evidence presented at the trial, the media had scrutinized every nuance, preference, and possibility of the doctor's actions and motives, all against the backdrop of the tragic death of one of the world's greatest musical superstars.

As the trial ensued, one fact remained unchanged in the face of all evidence presented: the charge of manslaughter. The charge of murder in any degree was never on the table. While I'm no court expert, the case seemed contingent on the issue of whether there had been gross negligence on the part of Dr. Murray, resulting in Michael's death, which thus led to the charge of manslaughter. The difference between this charge and one of murder is determined by the court's understanding of the doctor's intent.

Every doctor takes the Hippocratic oath as part of their certification to be a licensed physician. This vow includes "the promise to do no harm." It seems clear from the various testimonies and pieces of evidence that Dr. Murray never intended for MJ, or any of his patients for that matter, to die as a result of his treatment.

We know the esteemed cardiologist did not wake up that fateful morning and say, "I'm going to kill Michael Jackson today." The man's remorse has been apparent throughout the process. He was seen weeping on his way to sentencing even as he cried in certain moments of the trial. However, the guilty verdict delivered in the trial sends a message that Dr. Murray, despite his good intentions, must be held responsible for his involvement in his patient's overdose.

As we have seen in our excursion into the battle zone of unforgiveness, most of us end up hurt and maligned, wounded veterans of a war that continues to rage inside us even though the battle itself ended long ago. Most of us end up hurt by someone who wasn't even intending to hurt us, but their selfishness, egotism, and entitlement left us injured in the wake of their collateral damage, caught in the proverbial friendly fire of someone who claims to care about us.

Stranger at the Gate

Just as the impact of Michael Jackson's doctor, someone intending to care for his health, ended up contributing to Jackson's demise, we often get hurt by those who ostensibly want to help us. In many cases, we get bruised the most by people trying not to hurt us. No cheating husband sets out to break his wife's heart; it is the self-consumed fulfillment of his own need that drives him to be irresponsible regarding her reaction and well-being.

Most men who find themselves in an adulterous relationship with a woman did not decide one day that they wanted to see how badly they could break their wife's heart. Her heartache is simply one result of a husband who puts his own desires above all else. The fact that her pain emerges as collateral damage brings no comfort to the wife alone in her bed at night, crying herself to sleep over the husband who has betrayed her.

Parents who go through the trauma of divorce never intend to damage their children, and in fact usually do everything in their power to mitigate the upheaval and ease their children's transition. Fortunately, not all divorces have a negative impact on the children of couples who end their marriage. However, a parent's lack of malevolent intention cannot prevent some children from experiencing enormous wounds of fear, uncertainty, and feelings of abandonment.

So often, if we do not learn how to recover and restore our own sense of emotional health and well-being, then we become caught in a cycle that has a similar, viral impact on those around us. I have seen this played out in the life of a close family friend, a woman who babysat our children when they were small and worked closely with my wife in women's ministry. She is one of three sisters, and for a variety of reasons, she was not raised with the rest of her family. She has shared extensively with me about how her family would often come to visit her out of state where she lived with a cousin.

After a glimpse into the normalcy of having her sisters around her teasing and loving her, after a peek into what it would be like to have her parents present to hear about her day and celebrate her accomplishments, my friend would have to pull the curtain on such visions and return to the reality of their separation.

Whenever her family would leave, she would walk to the gate

and watch their car disappear down the street, watch the red glow of the car's taillights melt into the sea of traffic. That was the moment every time when she felt the full weight of being abandoned. She told me that she always fantasized that one day she would be standing there, waiting, her eyes brimming with tears, and then her family's car would turn around and come back for her, with her parents and sisters unable to endure her absence in their midst. Only her fantasy never came true and remained just that— the unfulfilled longings of a lonely girl's imagination.

My friend is successful, charming, smart, strong, and compassionate. She lights up a room and people like her. Her life appears to be one that you or I might envy, unless we knew that her heart is still at the gate. To this day, she finds it difficult to invest in relationships because she feels that if she brings her full self to the other person, then she risks being abandoned. So instead she doesn't make the proper investment to have a strong relationship with anyone. She allows herself to go only so far, metaphorically to the gate, before she detaches and withholds her ability to commit.

I've watched her date handsome men who were both strong and gentle. They are attracted to her vivacious personality and attractive figure, but once they begin to date her, they find that while the container is opulent, the box is empty. The contents of human character, love and connectivity, don't seem to exist in her.

Because I know her story and the fragility of her heart, I know differently. I see the small child trapped inside the body of a very beautiful woman who finds herself perpetually at the gate again, watching the car leave. Her fear of abandonment has become her master and she its slave, shackled by her unwillingness to connect with the strength of attachment necessary to build a healthy, trusting relationship. I cannot tell you how many disappointed, wounded men have been trampled over in the process of trying to

find someone to love them without ever knowing that they are seeing someone who is seeing them forever from the gate.

Whenever I read the biblical text about the lame man at the
gate called Beautiful, I think of my friend. We're told that a man
who had been lame since birth would have his friends carry him
to the gate called Beautiful, which was on the route to the Temple.
People on their way to worship or to make an offering would pass
by the lame beggar and give him money since he was unable to
work for a living.

One day Peter and John came along and the lame man called
out to them, asking for money. The two followers of Jesus probably
didn't have much to give because Peter said, "Silver or gold I do not
have, but what I do have I give you. In the name of Jesus Christ of
Nazareth, walk" (Acts 3:6, NIV). They offer the man a hand and
he gets up, walks, and then begins jumping and skipping around,
praising God for the miraculous gift of healing that had just de-
scended upon his ankles and feet.

The thing the lame man longed for most—the ability to walk
on healthy feet—was not something he allowed himself to ask for.
Begging for the spare change of churchgoers on their way to worship was much easier. Ironically, Peter and John could not give
him what he asked for—they tell him they don't have any silver or
gold—but they are able to give him what his heart had all but quit
hoping to one day discover.

Since he had been crippled from birth, he had never taken a
step without the debilitating pain shooting up through his ankles, into his calves, causing his weak legs to stumble. And now
suddenly he can walk—pain free! With the joyful abandonment of
a toddler just discovering the capacity for his two legs to carry him
forward with each step, this grown man experiences the mobility
for which his body was designed.

If only my friend could experience the same miracle that is just as available to her as it was for the lame man, then the rusty gate of her childhood at which she hovers could be transformed into a place of miracles, truly a gate Beautiful! She simply has to ask for what she wants and keep the passionate hope alive that she need not protect herself from the risk of loving.

And in order to ask, she must be willing to forgive, to realize that those who hurt her with their abandonment carry around their own painful scars of having been left behind at the gates of their own formative years. If you have ever been the victim of someone whose weaknesses have left you feeling murdered in heart, soul, or body, part of the healing begins when you understand that most perpetrators are themselves victims.

Wounded Warriors

Most people who have been injured in some way react to that wounding by unconsciously wounding other people. I categorize them in three types: 1. the **insulator;** 2. the **isolator;** and 3. the **inhibitor.**

The first responder, the insulator, wraps herself up in such a disguise that no one can access her heart and hurt her again. Like my friend who lingers at the gate of her childhood loss, the insulators hide within layers of emotional armor in an attempt to prevent anyone from ever seeing who they really are. They go to work wrapped in insulation; they get married in insulation; they interact with people at church through thick pads of insulation. It is not the individual with whom they find themselves conversing that they are committed to warding away, but it is the fear that what has happened in the past will inevitably occur again that causes them to smother all possibility for human intimacy.

To those of us who are very perceptive, when we encounter such individuals, we know that something about them does not ring true. We often label them as smooth or slick or deceitful and remain wary of them without knowing how to pinpoint the originating evidence for such a response. They send off a signal, often unintentionally, that communicates with those around them subliminally, making it clear not to get too close. Depending on the circumstance and kind of relationship, we may be wise to remain at arm's length.

However, if we take the time to peel away the layers of foam around the insulators, we find the layers are shielding the person out of fear. They cannot commit to other people because they remain committed to protecting the child within who has grown physically but remains dwarfed emotionally. No one knows that these persons live their lives as little boys with thumbs in their mouths, tears in their eyes, living, loving, dancing, and doing business from the gate of a traumatic experience that they say nothing about.

The second group is comprised of isolators: They isolate themselves to avoid the possibility of rejection. Unlike the insulators, who still engage in relationship, albeit beneath layers of protective padding, the isolators may stand before you but it's clear that they are not there with you. They have left their battered heart at home, removed from their day-to-day interactions. Like a patient in the intensive care unit, the isolator's emotional health may be so fragile that they do not want to risk taking the body of their pain off life support.

Isolators not only remain alone in a crowd, they are afraid to integrate into their environment for fear of a rejection that feels like it would trigger emotional annihilation. These self-saboteurs assume an attitude of isolation to remove the possibility that anyone might touch them or get too close. They do not feel comfortable around people, whether in large groups or one-on-one. Whether meeting strangers, communicating with people who think they know them well, or interacting with family and loved ones, isolators feel safest in a perpetual state of suspended dislocation.

This group of people breaks my heart the most because I understand, as the Bible said, it's not good for man to be alone. Their isolation is so pervasive that often these people are tortured in the presence of opportunities, intimidated in the presence of crowds only because their isolation requires constant vigilance. They have the misperception that solitariness is freedom. Their isolation continues to protect them from what they fear while also tormenting them by keeping them from what they need.

Isolators are like people who go to extreme measures to create a home-defense system—alarms, motion-sensor lights, remote cameras, laser triggers, guard dogs, all the things you'd expect a billionaire to put in place for his most exquisite mansion. Yet the isolator protects his house so securely that when he wants to welcome a visitor into his home, he doesn't know how to disable the elaborate systems put in place to thwart unwanted intruders.

They may have children, friends, coworkers, and other associates, but they remain in a state of guarded segregation, separated from others by their own defenses. I have seen countless people who committed suicide while all those around them were shocked. No one can understand why, the person seemed so gregarious, so nice, so polite, so pleasant. Those around them failed to detect that the deceased was always isolated and tormented, and finally could no longer endure their own self-induced solitary confinement.

Our third group, the inhibitors, responds to the wounding of others with a sense of pessimistic frustration that is unparalleled. Enough is never enough to make up for what they have lost, what they have endured, what they continue to carry around inside themselves. No matter what they attain or what they accomplish, they remain disappointed and trapped in a perpetual state of frustration.

They are frustrated because the good things in life seem to leak out of them, never lasting long enough to bring refreshment and quench their thirst. Like pouring water into a rusty bucket, no compliment, no encouragement seems to stay with them because it's leaking out through the holes of human wounds and personal discouragements that have never been repaired.

Even as they interact with people they love, their own sense of past injustice has birthed a present sense of entitlement that repels others. They attempt to find solace by making money, achieving another promotion, or reinventing their appearance with cosmetics, elaborate jewelry, and designer clothing. But no matter how good they look, they continue to inhibit their own growth by perpetually picking at the wounds of their past.

Bully for You

The alternative to turning inward and becoming ensnared as an insulator, isolator, or inhibitor is to turn your wounded rage outward and become a bully. You may not see yourself this way, but those around you know that you wield powerful weapons in your determination to make others submit to your power. Bullies grant no one forgiveness, castigating and maligning others to camouflage their own vulnerabilities. They prey on the weaknesses of everyone around them, exploiting them, manipulating them, controlling them, reminding them perpetually of their flaws.

Much has been said in recent days about the bullying we've seen in schools, playgrounds, locker rooms, and classrooms across America. According to research conducted by STOMP Out Bullying (www.stompoutbullying.com), one in four children has been bullied at school and 43 percent of kids have been bullied online. We've all heard horrific stories of heartbreaking loss about cyberbullies who spread malicious lies and poisonous gossip through the viral contagion of social media. These bullies intimidate other children because of their differences, whether it be their physical limitations, their weight, their gender, or their sexual orientation. This problem has become so horrendous that many victims of these bullies take their own lives to escape horrendous verbal or physical assaults.

We must correct this problem by teaching our children to respect and interact with others who are different in some way from ourselves. But let us be clear, that bullying doesn't just occur on playgrounds or in school systems, or as isolated behavior in hormonal adolescents. I have seen bullies in marriages, spouses who use domestic violence to slaughter the self-esteem of someone they say they love.

According to the Domestic Violence Resource Center (www.dvrc-or.org), one in four women in the United States will be physically assaulted in her lifetime by a spouse, boyfriend, or partner. Over three million women in our country will report physical injuries as a result of an abusive altercation with their husband or significant other. Keep in mind that this does not include the thousands of cases that go unreported, or the thousands who may not have physical wounds but who bear emotional and psychological scars from abuse.

Many people who have no direct experience with domestic abuse often find it hard to understand why so many women return to their abusers. Among several reasons, it is often difficult for these women to leave these men because they're often as charming as they are destructive. Many women don't seem to understand how to get the man they want without enduring the man they don't.

This behavior is not limited, however, to the male gender because I have often seen women who bullied men with their words just as powerfully as if it were with their fists. These women continually point out his defects and insufficiencies, never acknowledging his attributes and accomplishments. These female bullies in the home bring up past mistakes for years, using them as a club to batter and bruise their husband's masculinity and self-esteem until he is so fragmented as an individual that he lives as or assumes a deformed caricature of the man he would be.

After preaching hundreds of funerals over the course of my thirty-five years in ministry, I have seen amazing transformations that leave me and other mourners confused. Often I have witnessed the people who tormented the deceased when he or she was alive become the most distraught. They're wailing and telling stories about their relationship with the deceased, pulling flowers out of the way so they can get as close as possible to the casket. How amazing it is that those people who kill you can then cry the loudest because you're dead! Guilt often imitates grief in those who bully and torment other people.

It's not just our words and our fists we use as weapons. So many people in our narcissistic age of tweeting our every thought find they can bully others with their intellectualism. They assassinate the value of people of lesser intelligence, looking down their nose and belittling those who have not had the opportunity or taken the opportunity to use education to enhance their life. The fact remains that all of us are God's children, created in his glorious image. Even those with less intelligence can make just as valuable contributions of their own.

How foolish to think that because a person doesn't know everything, they don't know anything. Every chemist needs a lawn boy, every doctor needs a plumber, every CEO needs a mechanic. We are not independent of one another; we are interdependent. We drive away people that we ultimately need and then suffer for lack of what we could have had if we had not bullied people who were different from ourselves.

I know a guy who's a chemical engineer, respected and revered, brainy and brilliant. The other night he called me in a panic because his apartment was flooded and he didn't know what to do! He ended up losing a hundred grand worth of furniture because he, a near-genius-level chemical engineer, didn't understand what a pop-off valve is on a hot-water heater! There I am on the phone telling him to take a wrench and turn the valve! Out of all his vast knowledge, something that might seem basic to many of us had eluded his grasp. He knew a lot of things but he didn't know this!

I'm reminded of the story of Naaman in the Bible, a well-respected, successful captain in the Syrian army. His followers were gladiators and men of valor known by the upper echelon of Israel and Syria for their cunning and skill. As their leader, Naaman was highly regarded as a man of extreme strength and influence. In spite of these qualities, beneath his shiny armor, he kept a dangerous secret: he was a leper.

None of his battle acumen or military strategies could make up for his infirmity. Not until a maid, a little girl who had been captured in Israel and now served Naaman's wife, told him about a prophet from her homeland, Elisha, who could heal him through the power of God. She did not have the benefit of education and influence that he did—she was basically an indentured servant in his household—and yet he would have died, in spite of his strength and intelligence, without her (for the full story, see 2 Kings 5:1-19).

If in any way you see you're behaving as a bully in anyone else's life, I challenge you to correct whatever fuels your need to make yourself seem big by making someone else seem small. You need to understand that belittling another human being does not make you larger but draws attention to the fact that if you didn't think yourself smaller you wouldn't have to go to such lengths to look bigger at someone else's expense. You may not even realize the impact of your interactions, but bullying is wrong in every form, whether physical, verbal, or emotional. You may not have intended to hurt them, but whether by manslaughter or murder, the child remains under your car.

Good Intentions

Perhaps you recognized yourself as well as the people you love among these four types who struggle to recover and move on with the kind of productive, abundant life their Creator intended. So how do we break through the layers of emotional insulation, the elaborate defense systems around our heart, and our ineffective inhibitions? How do we stop the terrible transformation into bullies who find distorted relief by mimicking the abuse of their own perpetrators? I'm glad you asked, because the key lies in knowing that our recovery requires emotional exercise and spiritual mobility.

Like a patient recovering from a life-threatening automobile accident, we must push through our own pain in order to return to a state of healthy functionality. The speed with which we recover from our wounds is often directly proportional to our awareness of our own flaws and our willingness to move forward and risk again. We must learn how to forgive, and if not forget past offenses, then at least release their hold on us.

When a cardiologist runs a battery of tests to determine the strength and health of a patient's heart, he usually includes a treadmill test to determine how quickly the heart recovers from the exertion. Healthy hearts recover quickly, pumping much-needed oxygen-rich blood throughout the body, which has been depleted by the exercise. Our emotional hearts were also designed to help us recover quickly.

Unfortunately, they often become clogged and constricted with our anger, hurt, resentment, and bitterness. If we want to restore our emotional and spiritual health, then we must exercise forgiveness on a regular if not daily basis. Instead of driving us inward to insulate, isolate, or inhibit, our anger over having a weakened heart from an unexpected injury can become the fuel for our recovery.

I think what allows us to forgive people who have committed some kind of manslaughter in our lives is that we have taken the time to understand why they've done what they've done. It's very difficult to hate someone you understand. The Bible says in all things gain understanding. Earlier in my life, I often wondered what was so important about getting understanding. Of all things you can obtain, achieve, accomplish, and procure, the Bible repeatedly emphasizes the vital importance of understanding.

Having reached a point in my life where I understand this text now, it's clear that understanding not only helps you to sympathize, if not empathize, with another person, but it's also the powerful tool through which we can repair the damage. Through understanding, returning to the scene of the offense and standing under the person who has hurt us, we free ourselves by gain-ing insight into our perpetrator's intentions. We realize it was not deliberate murder they committed but incidental manslaughter.

And please allow me to be clear here in recognizing that in both cases, manslaughter or murder, a death occurs, something is lost that cannot be restored to life. When a father in his haste to get to work backs over his three-year-old child in the driveway, his careless accident is the last thing he ever intended. He leaps out of the car screaming in pain because he never saw how his actions would hurt someone he loved, and yet people do this in some way every day.

The tragedy of it all is that good intentions will not undo the life-threatening injuries incurred by the damaged child. The father's remorse does not remove the bruises, nor does it take away the scars. And yet if that child is ever to recover emotionally, his restoration is expedited when the child knows that Daddy never meant to hurt him.

Perhaps you have reached a point in your adult life where you can suddenly see your parents in a different light. Maybe you can now understand the pressures they were under, the stress heaped upon them, the wounds they themselves carried on their backs. Rare is the parent who does not at least attempt to do their best for their child, even if their best effort is limited beyond their control. Understanding what it was like for your mother, for your father, can free you to forgive them with a depth that finally goes to the roots of your own wounding. Let them go! Release them from the cage of painful memories and bitter disappointments and simply try to love them for what they did give you.

Let Them Go

My own personal understanding of my parents has certainly been enhanced by being a parent myself. For the record, I am a survivor . . . I have survived the challenging stage of life of raising adolescent children! It was a narrow escape! Many times I thought I would not make it. Many times I thought my children would not make it! This temporary state in the life of a human being that we call adolescence can produce some of the most insulting remarks known to man. How could someone who started out so sweet, cuddly, and cute end up being so selfish, so self-absorbed, and so vicious in their remarks? And yet it seems to be inherent to that season of life in which an individual separates himself and begins formulating his own identity apart from how his parents see him.

I survived it and you can survive it, too. The vindication comes after the child who complained endlessly about what a bad parent you were grows into adulthood and finds out that it's not as easy to be as perfect at parenting as they had assumed. Grandchildren are the vindication of bruised parents who now get to see their child empathize with the plight of parenthood. This is the stage of life when the greatest bonding between you and your child begins. Bonding that connects you is not a sign of how right you were. But rather it is the bonding that occurs when both parent and adult child share in the connectivity that comes from being mutually flawed.

When one assumes that one is without fault, it becomes so easy to stone another. But when those faults become so blatant and obvious that the rock of criticism flips from the hand of self-indignation, a humility ensues that becomes a tremendous vehicle for true forgiveness. My point is simple: He who is without fault among us, let him cast the first stone. Now, the details may be different but the truth is that all of us have hurt someone at some time in some way whom we did not mean to damage.

If we are to be forgiven, then we must be prepared to give forgiveness. We all know that if you live long enough, every human being will commit manslaughter, financially, maritally, relationally. It is our commonality with all human beings. If you can admit that you need forgiveness, then my question to you is why won't you give it?

It is my hope that every victim could find grace to forgive the perpetrator. I am certainly not suggesting that forgiveness requires continued exposure to ongoing abuse. This would be foolish as well as immensely dangerous. But understanding the sickness that drives a bully is a tremendous resource for freeing your heart from the pain of their assault.

Let them go so that you may be the one who experiences the same giddy freedom as the lame man at the gate called Beautiful. Let them go so that you can let yourself go!

ten
Mercy Me

One doesn't have to be clad in a black judicial robe or wield a gavel in his hand to find himself in a position of power. We do not have to be subpoenaed to a trial or summoned to jury duty to find ourselves deliberating about our response to another's plea for our mercy or forgiveness. Now, to be sure, sometimes penitence isn't enough to exonerate the guilty. Yes, there are times when doing the right thing requires that we stand against injustice or incompetence. We do others, as well as ourselves, no favor if we lower our standards to the point that we lose the integrity of what we are building as our legacy.

When we place our offender on trial, the question remains: Should we offer up our compassion on the altar of religious convictions and righteous principles, esteeming our ideals higher than the needs of the individual? The screams of the innocent people hanged during the Salem witch hunts echo across the centuries to remind us what happens when human ideals supersede justice.

Those who felt sure they were right when they were abominably wrong have killed countless souls.

Prior to DNA testing, who can tell us how many men died innocently while people celebrated gleefully thinking that justice had been served when in fact it had been aborted? They were sure they were right when they were indeed wrong. It is a telling statement when the psalmist David, who had sinned by counting his soldiers, brought judgment down on himself and others. Why did he choose, when given an option, to be placed into the hands of God rather than men? What is it about God's flawless character that made a guilty man choose divine justice over the verdict of other men just as flawed as himself? We have discussed forgiveness from many perspectives, but let's examine forgiveness from God's perspective and learn how it influences our own. As we will explore, those who practice forgiveness regularly often receive it regularly as well.

New Every Morning

At some point in our lives, usually as adults when we wake up the morning after one of our own offenses, we realize that we serve a forgiving God. If he weren't, then none of us would likely be here! Our God isn't just powerful and righteous, but he is also merciful and compassionate. It is not just that he acts mercifully toward us his children, but mercy is at the very heart of who he is. Any human can show mercy but such behavior does not reveal the essence of their character necessarily.

However, this isn't the case with God. He is in his Almighty being full of mercy. His mercies are so relentless that Jeremiah, one of his prophets, said of them, "They are new every morning" (Lamentations 3:23, KJV). We aren't left to face a new day with old mercy, or a fifty-fifty possibility of mercy. If this were the case, then such mercy would be inadequate and incompetent. The reason his mercy is new every morning is that yesterday's mercy removed all record of yesterday's mistakes so he is ready to start fresh again with us today.

He doesn't hold our mistakes over our head like people do. If God kept score, got even, or sought to settle old scores with us, we would all be in a grave condition and critical state of affairs. Now, to be sure, he is also a God of justice, and his mercy doesn't allow us the luxury of a flagrant disregard for his authority. Paul makes it clear when writing to the Christians in Rome that God doesn't want us to continue in a flagrant disregard for his wishes (Romans 6:1). No, God wants us to grow, to change and repent. Still his mercy is the defense attorney that releases us from the prosecuting attorney of his justice. When Justice said, "They deserve to die," Mercy pleaded our case and this is why you and I are here. His mercy is meant to be observed by us all that through our contemplation his divine nature might be revealed. We also see how fellowship with him has influenced our human behavior and affairs.

As a father I feel it is important that my children respect me, but I don't want to be such a disciplinarian that they shudder when my car pulls in the driveway. Our Heavenly Father, who also seeks a healthy relationship with his children, offers us mercy so that he can be more to us than our God, our Ruler, our Master, though he is all of these indeed. Our Creator also longs to have that more intimate relationship with us. He longs to be revered as our Father and not just our moral policeman. Understanding this dimension of God's character and how he expresses it to us forms a bedrock foundation for our understanding of forgiveness.

Unfortunately, many people never make this transition in

their understanding of God. They say they believe that there is a "Supreme Being," but they often do not take that far more intimate step into understanding that the Creator of the Universe is also their loving Father. They are terrified of the one who loves us unconditionally because such a response to our immorality is irrational.

God doesn't withhold his love until we are mature and developed. Instead he lavishly commends his love while we are yet sinners to show us the one real taste of unconditional love from the one source entitled to judge us that doesn't. He wants us to see that he who has every right to judge us but doesn't also expects some replication of his kindness extended toward others. As an act of contrition based on being a recipient of such amazing grace and kindness, our mercy then displays God's love to others.

Trickle Down

When we refuse to forgive, we basically insist on setting our standards higher than God's. Instead of being a conduit of his mercy, we who have often received it then deny it in a false sense of piety and religious purity. One of the stories that Jesus used to teach this essential truth does not seem to make it into very many sermons that I've heard these last few years. Perhaps this is why we are so painfully void of mercy and deficient of his kindness to others beyond our own family and selves. We lose sight of sharing, discussing, receiving, and extending forgiveness as a community.

We often hear about having a "trickle-down economy" from political leaders, referring to the wealth holders' releasing their money into the economy, which sets off a chain reaction through the various socioeconomic sectors. While this theory of economics may be flawed as a financial system, it is divinely accurate when applied to mercy. I believe you'll understand what I mean as we explore this fascinating parable.

This story involves a slave who was so indebted to his owner and so behind in his payments that the frustrated master decrees that the slave, his wife, his children, and all possessions be sold to recoup the losses incurred from the slave's flagrant failure to honor their agreement. When the slave hears this declaration, he weeps before the master in such an emotional outburst that ultimately the master's anger subsides. Impressed by the intensity of the slave's remorse, the compassionate master forgives the servant of his transgressions and extends to him grace and "forgave him of his debt" (Matthew 18). The servant is elated and the debt is forgiven and all is well.

However, as Jesus continues the story he says that the *same* servant who had been forgiven such a mammoth debt, barely escaping the annihilation of his family and the distribution of his possessions, walks away and encounters a fellow slave who happens to owe him some money. It's actually nothing compared to what the first slave owed his master, sort of like pennies to millions. Now, you would think that the first slave, in an act of celebratory gratitude, would extend to the one vulnerable before him the same compassion and mercy. Instead, though, the slave became enraged with his debtor and "grabbed him by the throat and started to choke him." I know this sounds a bit over the top, even unbelievable. But before you dismiss such a dramatic detail as cotton padding added to Matthew's gospel to raise the word count, might I ask you a question? *Have you been as merciful to others as God has been to you?*

When you and I consider how much God (who knows everything there is to know about us) still forgives us, covers us, and keeps us, how can we then find within ourselves the audacity to condemn others? Often pronouncing judgment without the slightest reflection on our own past and his kindness toward us, we flagrantly disregard God's gift to us as if we suffered from spiritual amnesia. "Who, me? Well, I've never done anything as bad as what he did to me!" or "I know exactly what God thinks of her behavior!" You do?

The slave had a chance to be important in the life of the slave who owed him. Isn't his indignant rage that resulted in the choking of another slave who was lacking the ability to pay him an attempt to medicate his low self-esteem with his self-aggrandizement? Perhaps I have judged the first slave wrongly. But I can't help but see traces of an arrogance far too often exhibited among those who desperately seek a chance to be the juror in order to escape the seat of the defendant.

Be Careful What You Pray For

Jesus's parable about the wretched slave who is forgiven but cannot forgive does not serve as our only glimpse into this vital principle of forgiveness. When his ravenous disciples feel the pangs of spiritual hunger and cry out to Jesus requesting him to teach them to pray, he complies and gives the template of prayer that we refer to as the Lord's Prayer. This beautiful, poetic prayer has such power and its language swells like an ancient, eternal anthem filled with theological glimpses into what is important to God himself. Like the daily bread included in its lines, the prayer itself is given as nourishing sustenance for our hungry souls.

Most striking is that in the midst of prayer Jesus includes a line that should make even the most pious of us shrink to our knees in disgrace over our own hypocrisy. Perhaps it has not bothered you before, but it has often haunted me like shadows dancing in the night outside of a five-year-old's bedroom window. Most of us have heard these famous words and many of us have quoted them and memorized them. But have you ever considered what these words actually mean? "Forgive us our trespasses as we forgive those who trespass against us." Oh my God! This is a frightening request. This simple statement ties my forgiveness with my willingness to forgive. Not as a condition—no, that would repudiate the essence of mercy that is at the heart of God's character. No, I believe this prayer reminds us of the way our hearts work. If we are not humbled with unwavering gratitude for what we have been forgiven, then it will be incredibly difficult for us to forgive other people what they do to us. It's difficult to teach someone else to ride a bike if you have always ignored your own dependence on training wheels!

Perhaps this is the key to feeling forgiven. People who do not feel forgiven often confront me. Many times they can't imagine a God so perfect forgiving a man so filthy. An unimaginable grace is often inconceivable to someone who fails to allow God's forgiveness to flow through themselves. They may try desperately to work for something that God gives for free, knowing all too well that they will not dispense what they are hoping to earn as compensation for their own sins.

We often pray, "Forgive us our trespasses as we forgive those who trespass against us." But are we really prepared to have God treat our own foolishness the same way we treat others? There have been times in my life that I struggled to say those words when the Lord's Prayer is being quoted. In truth, I absolutely wanted God to handle me differently than I was willing to treat others who violated me or broke their word to me. I had to learn to extend the same mercy to others that I would want myself.

Perhaps one of the reasons we are allowed by God to be trespassed against by others in the first place is to give us an opportunity to demonstrate his love to others who are in need of our mercy. If this is true, then it is critical to our spiritual well-being that we discover the grace space in which God exists so that we can dwell with him by exemplifying his character even when our own is so lacking. Yes, it is easier to be judgmental regarding the foolishness in someone else's behavior than it is to confront our own. Could it be possible that what has happened to us is just a test? Why do the forgiven fail to be forgiving?

Power Trip

An opportunity for you to forgive an offender is not so much a test of how you handle power as it is how you handle mercy. The difference between the offended and the offender is often a thin line with only a nuance of distinction between participating parties.

This feeling of superiority can be intoxicating. It reminds me of the banks who sought a bailout from the government during the recent recession. CEOs and bank presidents sheepishly appeared before Congress asking for financial mercy and debt relief. And we all stood in shock because once these lenders were in financial compliance with their obligations, they who had received the government's help then refused to help those whose mortgages were in arrears with their institutions!

When those who were brought low get up, they eventually have to face the test of how they will handle a position of power. This may be the greatest test of anyone's character. We saw it played out on a national stage as begging bankers transformed in a matter of days back into belligerent bankers. Millions of people who had always lived in homes and paid bills in a timely manner were tossed to the streets, leaving them in homeless shelters with their children in tow, and the banks turned their backs and flew to the next board meeting in their private jets without even the slightest attempt to help single mothers and working dads who only wanted them to forgive as they had been forgiven, to help as they had been helped. The banks failed the test. No doubt many of us have failed it, too. It is the test of being in control, on top, in power!

It's not just a test of how you do business, of course. The more intimate the relationship, the more personal the stakes become. Peter warns husbands, who had been charged by him and the apostle Paul to lead their wives and households, to avoid taking their power so far that they lose their sense of compassion and become "inconsiderate" to the vulnerability of their spouses. He writes, "Husbands, in the same way, treat your wives with consideration as the weaker partners and show them honor as fellow heirs of the grace of life. In this way nothing will hinder your prayers!" (1 Peter 3:7, NIV).

That "nothing will hinder your prayers" sounds ominous, almost threatening. It seems that God does care how you handle power when it is given or appointed. Now, whether you agree with Peter's assertion that the woman is the weaker partner, you have to at least realize that women in his day were basically reduced to the equivalent of property in marriage. It wasn't just their ancient, unenlightened culture, but in our own country and around the world, women had absolutely no rights, could not vote, own property, or lead a business. In many cultures women were and are still sold to men like slaves. Yet God speaks up for the underprivileged and warns that the one in power has an obligation to be considerate in how we treat those with whom we have power.

Call me foolish, but I would rather err on the side of mercy than become consumed with the arrogance of self-righteousness and fail to offer the benefit of grace that I have also received. Yes, there have been times I have had to make unpopular decisions and have been forced to maintain the integrity of our church or company by disciplining or terminating an employee. But this is for me the most agonizing of decisions, as I know that God is watching, and as Jesus said in the Beatitudes, "Blessed are the merciful for they shall obtain mercy!"

Rock Your World

Perhaps the most powerful example of forgiveness in the Bible is also the most salacious (John 8). If this incident had been filmed, the rating for the video would go far beyond what most Christians would endorse, and yet this is a situation described by Jesus himself. It is the story of a woman snatched from the sweaty sheets of her illicit lover's bed. Whenever I read this story I imagine her chest still heaving, hair in disarray, and her pulse heightened as this woman's warm, sensuous body is yanked from her lover's caress by the forceful hands of an angry religious mob.

Dragging her down the cobblestoned streets of Jerusalem without allowing her the benefit of bathing or dressing, the crowd is fueled by disgust, their rage blinding them, their righteous indignation demanding that something be done to restore dignity to their holy dominions of ecclesiastical power. Her knees bruised from their roughness, her eyes wide with fear, the adulteress is brought nude and humiliated down to the public square so that she may be stoned for her improprieties.

Isn't it interesting that they left the man in his domain, curled up in his warm bed, free from the same ridicule as the woman? One of the tragedies of men in power is that they have mercy on one and murder the other, making deals and selling pardons for the right price. And yet, if justice isn't blind can there be justice at all? No one asked themselves this question as they hurled insults at the woman caught in adultery and screamed for her blood to be shed. They had no mercy for a woman with no defense since those present had all witnessed her weakness. Nor did they reflect that they themselves had been a recipient of mercy, a divine mercy that they now refused to allocate to this woman who desperately needed the same.

When people witness your weakness, it gives them so much power over you. But the issue is not having power. The question, you'll remember, is what would you do with that power? Jesus brought it home and made it real when he told the snarling religious mob, "Let he who is without sin cast the first stone." One by one the crowd dispersed until none of her accusers were present. She was clearly guilty and scripturally inexcusable, and yet Jesus told her that since no one else was there to accuse her, then he would not accuse her, either. He told her to go and sin no more, not expecting her to be perfect from then on but rather always mindful of the grace she had received. In other words, we should learn from our mistakes, not crawl back into bed with them!

Without a doubt, I know God watches those of us who have influence and authority to monitor the way we extend the mercy and kindness that we also enjoy. The Bible says what measure you meet shall be met unto you again! In other words, your deeds will be weighed on the same scale in which you weigh others'. Recall Peter's strong warning to the husband that God will hinder his prayers from being answered if he abuses his authority and refuses to honor his wife. Thus, a consequence of unanswered prayer could be an indication of his judgment on us when our judgment isn't up to par with how we treat others.

I have seen people of faith who live moral lives contribute to the work of God and yet they seem unable to live in the abundant flow of what they should have from God. These people are often perplexed when their prayers seem unanswered. Often they will question God's ability or even his existence when they face disappointment. But they fail to look at whether they have complied with grace and mercy in their human affairs. It could very well be possible that they have blocked their own blessing by an attitude of cynicism.

I challenge you to wipe the slate clean and align yourself up so that all the blessings that are meant for you aren't hindered or blocked by the way in which you forgive others who trespass against you. It would be a sad thing to miss countless promised blessings simply because you held a grudge and missed the chance to receive what you need because of some unresolved offense!

No Second Chances

If you consistently experience God's mercy on a daily, ongoing basis, then you know that there are no second chances. There are *infinite* chances. While we must act like the forgiven sons and daughters we are, his mercies remain new every morning. When we act accordingly, then our mercies that we extend to others become just as fresh.

Sometimes we experience a trial or ordeal that reminds us what it's like to be given another chance. I have a dear friend who unwittingly entered into business with someone who was targeted by the FBI for his unscrupulous business tactics. Before long my friend was also indicted and a long and expensive court battle ensued.

Eventually when the time came for my friend to stand trial, he was as nervous as a cat in the dog pound. While it was clear that my friend had been duped into a position that compromised his integrity and made him vulnerable to a ten-year prison sentence, we could not count on his vindication. There was no question that he had an alliance with the parties in this terrible business deal. But he had entered into it without knowing that his new partner's resources were gotten through illegal gain.

His lawyer spoke eloquently, but my friend requested to testify and he tearfully threw himself on the mercy of the court. After some careful deliberation, the judge vindicated my friend, giving him a strong warning. I will never forget the sound of joyful relief in his voice when he called me to announce that his case had been dismissed! Usually reserved and solemn, my friend sounded like a high school girl going to the prom as he gushed about how the judge had given him a second chance at making better choices. I could hardly understand what he was saying as he exclaimed, "The charges have been dropped and I have been exonerated!" Sounding like he had just hit the lifetime jackpot in Vegas, his joy was a direct result of being forgiven.

This kind of freedom isn't valued by most of us until an incident challenges our liberty. To be given a second chance is a feeling that defies expression. This feeling is essential for those who recognize our own guilt is freely forgiven, not because we are blameless but because of God's mercy. Like my friend, many of us who could have been held to the letter of the law are in fact given a precious gift of mercy.

If you have been forgiven you are richer than the wealthiest person in the world. What a magnificent blessing it is to know that you are free! My friend no longer had to wonder who was following him. No more nervous quivers when the phone rang. No more anxiety when the doorbell chimed. There's an emotional euphoria in knowing that the weight of your transgressions has been lifted from your shoulders. There is a joy in knowing you have been forgiven. It is a joy that I pray you bask in and nurture, resting in the grace of our God who could rightfully judge us but who continually chooses to extend his mercy toward us.

If you have been forgiven there is no need to walk in guilt. Choose rather to walk in the wisdom that avoids foolish repetitions of the same mistake made over and over again. There is only one other thing that God requires of those of us who have been forgiven. That is that we also in similar fashion extend that grace in how we handle others.

eleven

Love Thy Neighbor As Thyself

A business associate of mine, a man who became a good friend over time, shared with me a vital lesson he learned about himself in a way he will never forget. As an up-and-coming entrepreneur in the world of social media marketing, this gentleman poured everything he had into getting his company off the ground—eighteen-hour days, weekend overtime, and constant networking to get the buzz going on what his company could provide. After the first year, his firm had blossomed into a leader in the field, and in order to keep up with the needs of his growing clientele, he added a dozen new employees. Soon they moved into a beautiful suite of offices in one of the most upscale neighborhoods near the downtown area of his city.

Year two produced numerous challenges, and most of them were surmountable and easily resolved. However, as his company entered its third year, my friend reached a business plateau and couldn't figure out why his firm seemed to have stopped growing. Projects and clients were steady but new ones weren't coming in at the pace they once had. So my friend did everything he knew to do, even restructuring the company into a more efficient organizational management paradigm. Six months later, still no new growth, and the plateau was starting to give way to a drop-off.

Panicked, my friend used his network and talked to other experts in the media and entertainment industries. Several contacts recommended the same independent consultant to come in and assess the problem and offer possible solutions. After contacting the consultant, the distraught entrepreneur wondered what this outsider, whose services didn't come cheap, could possibly tell him about his own company, an entity that he had brought from its infancy as nothing more than a spark of an idea to its current fruition of a respected, profitable business employing fifty people and serving over two hundred clients.

The consultant came in and spent a week interviewing various employees as well as a few clients. The second week, the consultant followed my friend around and took copious notes throughout every meeting or corporate function at which the CEO was required. At the end of the two weeks, the consultant met with the business owner and told him, "Your problem is simple, but it will require more from you than you've ever given this company if you want to rekindle its growth."

My friend looked both relieved and worried at the same time, he later told me. "Go on," he said to the confident-sounding troubleshooter, "please tell me." The woman looked him in the eye, smiled, and said, "Sir, with all due respect, *you* are the problem here. You are in the way of your own success. Until you move out of the way, your company will never grow."

Dumbfounded and reactively defensive, my friend kept his

cool and asked her to explain. She summarized how his strengths of innovation, networking, and relational leadership had made his social media firm successful, but now that the company had reached a certain size, the company president and founder spent all of his time weighed down by meetings, administration, and management challenges. He no longer had time to do what had made his company successful in the first place!

Without a doubt, my friend knew she was right, and based on her recommendation, he hired a top-notch MBA-trained executive to serve as president and chief operating officer while he would become the chief imagination officer and return to what he did best. Within three months of this new arrangement, my friend's business began booming and now shows no sign of slowing down anytime soon. He had been standing in his own way and never saw it until someone pointed it out to him.

Love Thy Neighbor

Unfortunately, I believe we often stand in the way of our own success, both personally and professionally, just like my friend discovered. Instead of being distracted by administrative challenges that cripple creativity, many of us find ourselves consumed by self-contempt and diverted from allowing our gifts to be used as God intended by our unwillingness to forgive ourselves. We repeatedly fail to extend forgiveness to the one person who needs it the most, the one person who desperately cries out for mercy and grace on a daily basis. Some of us not only ignore this person's request for compassion and understanding, but we berate this individual as unworthy of such kindness and consideration.

Yes, sometimes we are our own worst enemy when it comes to forgiveness. We may be willing to forgive other people, even those who may have committed the most heinous offenses against us, and yet we carry around thousand-pound packs of resentment, anger, frustration, and even hatred toward ourselves. Some people tell me that they end up feeling guilty and ashamed of not being able to forgive themselves, further complicating this internal drama that can grip us like a deadly vise that squeezes us tighter and tighter by our own hand.

This snare is not only debilitating, but it goes against the admonition we are given in God's Word about how we are to relate to others as well as ourselves. Both in the Old and New Testaments of the Bible, we are told that God's fundamental rule about how we are to interact with one another can be summed up, "Love thy neighbour as thyself" (Leviticus 19:18, KJV). In fact, out of hundreds and hundreds of Jewish laws about behavior and godly conduct, Jesus said that all of the laws basically relied on only two of them, to love God with all our heart, soul, mind, and strength, and to love our neighbor as we love ourselves (Mark 12:30–31, Matthew 22:37–39).

The assumption that most people bring to this Golden Rule is that we all know we love ourselves and know how we want to be treated so therefore we should love others and treat them the same way. However, many people do not seem to have this basic, healthy love for themselves, which in turn makes it nearly impossible for them to love others any better. If they can't love themselves, then how can they express anything resembling unconditional love to anyone else? It is difficult to impossible to teach someone else something that you have never experienced firsthand yourself.

This dynamic explains why so many people have a hard time forgiving others and extending them mercy because they are unable to receive the grace God gives them and let go of the standard of perfection to which they hold themselves accountable. If our neighbor suffers from our unforgiveness as a result of our own self-contempt, then we are doubly punishing ourselves and them. Scripture makes it clear that we are commanded to love others as God loves us, and this exhortation includes loving ourselves—no matter how difficult this may be.

Burning Down the House

I have not struggled with forgiving myself the way some people seem to punish themselves. Much of this freedom I experience is the result of coming from a loving home, where I knew without a doubt that I was loved unconditionally. Performance-based love is foreign to me and my experiences, and the more people I am around and the more stories I hear of their upbringing and dysfunctional home life growing up, the more grateful I am in realizing the priceless value of this rare commodity. I was far from being a perfect child, but I learned that no matter how much my mistakes cost, they never affected my priceless worth.

One of my childhood experiences illustrates this sense of love and acceptance in a vivid and unique way. My father was ill and required dialysis several times a week as I was growing up. My mother worked to help support our family, and so many of the domestic chores and caretaking for my father often fell on my young shoulders, including cooking many of our meals. I'll never forget the time when I almost set the house on fire but came away with a much more incendiary message burned into my mind.

Preparing a meal for me and my father, I had placed a big cast-iron skillet on the front burner of the stove with a little oil in it to fry some potatoes. I must have had the burner turned too high, and as I was distracted peeling and slicing my spuds the oil caught on fire. When I turned around and caught sight of what looked like a four-alarm fire there in our kitchen, I grabbed a dishtowel to use to pick up the burning skillet so I could take it to the sink or outside or anywhere away from the source of heat that was fueling its conflagration. Now, the dynamic phenomenon about fire that I did not take into consideration is that when you move forward with something burning, the onrush of air causes the flame to bend back toward the source of movement—in this case, ME!

As I struggled to lift the heavy skillet filled with a mini-Towering Inferno, the blaze bent back toward me and burned my hand and attempted to ignite my shirt. Immediately, I reacted to both the sight and more significantly the fiery sensation of being burned and possibly consumed by this kitchen catastrophe, and I dropped the skillet to the floor. With my hand stinging and reactively swollen right away, I knew I had just made matters about as bad as they could be, short of literally burning down the house.

Now, it would have been nice if that flaming skillet had fallen on an old, ratty throw rug or on tile or something that was not flammable. However, we had just gotten new carpet in our kitchen and dining room, an interior improvement that came with much saving, sacrificing, and selection-savvy on my parents' part. Needless to say, the black charred half circles of a cast-iron skillet were not part of the original design pattern of our new floor covering.

My father was livid, as any parent might be tempted to be, at what he considered my carelessness and failure to handle the problem differently. And certainly there were numerous ways I could have handled the kitchen fire in a better, calmer, more satisfactory method in order to extinguish it. I could have poured baking soda on it, or placed the skillet's lid on it before moving it from the stove, or smothered it with a blanket, or grabbed the portable fire extinguisher from the kitchen.

Considering my father's reaction to my accident, needless to say I was not looking forward to my mother's return from work at the end of the day. However, I was pleasantly surprised to see the way she downplayed it as one of those accidents that sometimes happen and focused instead on making sure that I was okay and that the burn on my hand was indeed a minor one needing no further medical attention. Now, she wasn't happy that her new kitchen carpet had a very noticeable, ugly burn mark where I had dropped the skillet. But she was grateful that the carpet had not managed to catch on fire as well and burn half the house down, and even more thankful that I was not seriously injured in the incident.

She and my father even argued about the situation, but my mother made it clear that in the grand scheme of things, this was something about which to be thankful and not resentful. She made it clear that this was an accident stemming from a mistake I made. I was not the mistake.

I've learned that all of us make mistakes in life. Good people sometimes do bad things. More than burning the kitchen rug. Things like having an abortion, telling off a coworker and losing their job, gambling away their life savings, backing over their child . . . The reality is the same, intentionally or unintentionally, whether it's manslaughter or murder, the other person is still dead.

We must learn to move forward without dragging our past mistakes behind us. We must reidentify ourselves as to who we are at the core of our being, who God created us to be, not who we are in our worst moments. So many people aren't even willing to allow their good moments, the times when they love those around them selflessly and charitably, to define them and instead focus only on their weaknesses, their flaws, their shortcomings and failures. No matter how many mistakes we've made, the reality is that we have more days ahead of us in which to be our truest selves.

"Sticks and stones" may indeed break our bones, but the names that we—or anyone else for that matter—throw at ourselves need not hurt us. The truth of the matter is that we are accepted and loved by God the same way. We are his Beloved and there's nothing we can do or not do to change the way he feels about us. However, we can do something about the way we feel about ourselves and the ways we tend to identify ourselves.

Better Than the Worst

While I have realized that I am most fortunate in not struggling with self-forgiveness (and some people would say that perhaps I should struggle with it more!), I know that many people live in anguished torment over the way they see themselves and keep their past mistakes ever before their eyes. For us who are Christians, it would be wonderful to think that we do not experience this issue as much as anyone else. However, I am grieved that so often we shoot our wounded in the church and only reinforce the false, negative opinion that the individual already carries about themselves.

I have seen this kind of situation played out in many different ministries, and I have always tried to show as much grace as possible to others, both within my church as well as beyond, who are struggling with issues of immorality and self-forgiveness. A recent situation has made me rethink the way the church usually responds to its leaders who fail.

One of the pastors on my staff has struggled with moral failures for much of his adult life. He has a beautiful wife, wonderful kids, and a clear anointing to minister powerfully to those around him. Yet he continues to act out in ways that he knows he ultimately does not want to act. His pattern is to indulge himself in something that he knows is wrong and clearly outside of the boundaries of commitment to his marriage and his ministry, not to mention his own sense of integrity. Then he will either reach a point and confess, or else he will be discovered in a compromising situation.

Amid many tears and heartfelt conversations, he repents and works hard to show himself as the man we all know and love and value. His wife would forgive him, our church team of other ministers and I would forgive him, and he would honor our faith in him. Then in roughly a year's time, he will go back to his divided life and secret sins until the process repeats itself. After several such cycles over a four- or five-year period, I knew we had to try something different. We had to get to the root of the problem in a way that radically altered the vicious cycle in which this good man kept himself stuck.

Without going into too many details, the change in response that we tried with my friend was to have what I like to call an "affirmation intervention." While he was in a season of doing well and not acting out to our knowledge, I arranged for a special meeting. His family and close friends, along with some other pastors with whom he was closest, gathered to surround him and tell him why we loved him so much, not for what he did for any of us—which in itself would be cause—but just because of his personality, his style, his uniqueness, his gifts of creativity and ministry, his loving nature, his strength and compassion. No one had to exaggerate or say anything other than the truth. At the same time, none of us mentioned his past indiscretions, moral failures, or weaknesses of character. Instead we focused on reminding this man of who he really is and why he is so easy to love.

At first he was taken aback and seemed as agitated as a wild animal placed in a cage, but once he realized that we really were there just to celebrate him and to remind him of the truth about himself, his demeanor changed dramatically. The defensive gaze and stiff body language immediately relaxed, and as each person took a turn describing their favorite qualities of him, he lowered his head and tears poured from his faith like a waterfall. For over an hour, he sat and wept and listened to this nuclear dose of affirmation.

Later, as he and I met to discuss and debrief his response to our special meeting, this pastor told me things about himself that he had never told me before, about horrific abuse as a child at the hands of both his parents, about childhood messages that he accepted upon himself as true that couldn't be further from it, about teenaged mistakes that in his mind only proved how terrible he was. It was clear that these many wounds had created a huge hole in this man's soul, a cumulative spiritual and emotional injury that he kept trying to numb and anesthetize with his immoral behavior while at the same time reinforcing the negative way he saw himself.

His need to be affirmed and validated, to be reminded of who he really is, had created an enormous vacuum in his heart. While there's no excuse for his failures and he remains responsible for the consequences of his decisions and actions, he recognized that there was more going on than just a battle with lust. It was only after he began to articulate the pain that he had carried for so long and to grieve the abuse suffered that he began to find freedom from the intensity of his addictive desires. He found himself finally receptive to God's healing touch in his life in ways that he had never been able to receive before. He knew he was a new creature in Christ just as we are told in the Bible (2 Corinthians 5:17) but had not been living out of his new identity until he made peace with his old one.

The same is true for you. You are better than the worst thing you have ever done. You are not who you once were nor who you will be tomorrow. Your life is a work of art in progress from the Masterpiece Maker of the Universe. He knew what he was doing when he created you and began the first brushstrokes of your life. And since it is a collaborative work, since he loves us enough to give us the freedom to choose what our painting will look like, he allows us to choose colors and images that he would not have chosen for us, and then to make them part of his design in a breathtaking way that we could never have imagined—let alone created—if left to our own way.

You see, God knows every secret you've got—the stolen money, the steamy chat room sessions online, the stash of prescription painkillers, the unwanted pregnancy, the illicit affair, the toxic gossip. On and on, he already knows it all. And still loves you! If he knew you were going to make all these mistakes and take all these wrong turns and go places he never would've wanted you to go and yet still loves you and blesses you, then you need to quit judging yourself and condemning yourself to a false identity.

So often people confess their mistakes to me and find themselves shocked that I don't run screaming out of the room when I hear the dirty, kinky, terrible, unimaginable, unspeakable, sinful thing they've done. They're even more shocked sometimes to hear that it's something that I've done before, too! Or at least to learn that they are not the only ones, that so much of what they have used to condemn themselves as unlovable and unpardonable is simply part of being human.

Once again, we come back to the essence of God's grace and his unmerited favor. All of us are imperfect and making mistakes and going off course, and our job is not to correct ourselves and get every aspect of our life lined up in perfect order for divine inspection. No, we simply have to receive the love God gives us like a child receives recess! Have you ever seen small kids bouncing like a group of puppies as they are about to be released from their studies into the freedom of the jungle gym and swing sets?

Children don't linger in the classroom, sulking and saying, "I can't go outside and play today—I don't deserve it. I'm just a terrible kid who should just sit in the corner while everyone else has fun on the playground." They run outside into the sunshine, laughing and racing to play with a joyful abandon that's undeterred by whether or not they got a gold star on their homework.

Inside Out

So how do we begin the process of self-forgiveness, especially if we have tried and failed in the ongoing process yet again? I'm glad you asked, because I was recently struck with a glimpse into how the healing process works while reading one of my favorite blogs. My daughter Sarah is a talented writer and gifted artist and frequently shares her insights on life, faith, and women's issues in her blog. Recently, she posted an entry regarding some medical and scientific research she had done on human skin and the way it heals from injuries, lacerations, and burns. Usually, we tend to think about scabs and scars as evidence of healing from such trauma to the epidermis, but what Sarah discovered is that healing begins from the inside out.

As soon as our skin is broken, our body's natural immune system triggers the release of extra white blood cells in our bloodstream to provide additional oxygen to the site of the wound as well as the rest of our body. Blood flow also increases dramatically at the point of injury in order to flush out germs, dangerous debris, and any foreign matter that might attempt to enter through the open wound and infect the rest of the body. This is why it feels like you can never stop bleeding when you cut yourself; your body is just doing its job.

The blood then coagulates around the entry wound in an attempt to seal and protect it, forming a scab that will then be replaced by a new layer of skin. Our body directs collagen particles there at the wound site in order to form new skin, usually lighter colored and more delicate than the surrounding skin, and which we usually call scar tissue.

We usually think about healing taking place due to the external treatment of the wound—stopping the bleeding, cleaning the wound, covering it with antibiotic ointment, and bandaging it with gauze or some other appropriate dressing. In actuality, however, the healing process immediately begins inside and must originate there if true wellness is to be restored. Some people try to pretend that everything is all right on the outside when they are secretly dying on the inside. They wear the right clothes and make sure their hair and makeup are flawlessly beautiful even as their eyes betray the pain that they're carrying around inside themselves.

No external makeover can change the essence of a person if they aren't willing to see themselves differently, accurately, the way God sees them. External beauty flows from internal harmony. Just as our body begins its healing triage reflexively, flushing out our wound and bringing extra nutrients to the injury, so we must wash away the sin that so easily entangles us and bring extraordinary compassion to ourselves. Even if you don't believe that you can do it, you must at least attempt to allow God to do it supernaturally. In fact, you don't have to do anything at all, simply receive, simply get out of your own way—and God's.

I'm here to tell you that no matter how unlovable, worthless, or hopeless you may feel, God knows everything about you, frontward and backward, and not only likes what he sees, but LOVES what he sees in you. Your secrets are not secrets to God, and his ways are not your ways. Once God gives you a gift or calling, he does not change his mind. He knew what you were going to do with it or not do with it long before you got to the place where you are currently. We are God's creation, his garment of praise that carries his divine designer label, and we can never remove his presence from who we are no matter what we have done.

In order to facilitate the healing process, you must change the way you think about yourself. Old tapes must be cut and destroyed so that new music can enter your soul. For many people, in order to make the leap from changing the way they think about themselves to changing the way they behave, they need community and a support network.

It might be counseling or a recovery group or perhaps volunteering at a shelter or facility that serves those who might be struggling with the same message you once owned as your identity. If you aborted your baby earlier in your life, then maybe you can share your story with young women wrestling with the same temptation. If you've kept a terrible family secret, then it's time you told someone who will be trustworthy and respectful of the burden you need to share. When you change your thoughts and beliefs, then it makes it easier to develop new patterns that will foster a healthy identity that reflects your true worth as a priceless son or daughter of the King of Creation.

If you agree with me that God does not make mistakes, then you must acknowledge that his making you—no matter how many mistakes you have made—is not an error on his part. Just as my mother told me when I burned the kitchen carpet with the hot skillet, you make mistakes but you are not the mistake. God knew you before the creation of the world and loves you with the tenderness that a mother loves her newborn. You cannot shock him or keep him from loving and forgiving you. It's time to let yourself receive the fullness of his grace and move on with your life. It's time to get out of your own way and allow yourself to grow beyond what you can even imagine. It's time to love—and forgive—thy neighbor as thyself.

twelve
Uprooted

I have been privileged to travel around the world and experience some of the most amazing gardens of various international cultures. I'll never forget taking in the natural beauty of South Africa's diverse landscape for the first time. With Table Mountain looming in the distance and Cape Town nestled nearby, Kirstenbosch National Botanical Garden offers over seven thousand species of indigenous African flora. Magnificent flocks of birds-of-paradise bloom next to jade plants, wild red orchids decorate the borders of miniature savannas, and brilliant blue irises rival the cerulean sky in the intensity of their hue. Established in 1913, it is the first botanical garden in the world established as the home of all of its native culture's plants, flowers, trees, and bushes.

While in Australia, I marveled at the Victoria State Rose Garden with its more than five thousand varieties of my mother's favorite flower. There I found more colors of roses than I knew existed in nature and such poetic descriptions of those colors—lavender moon, ivory cream, blood scarlet, sunburst orange, and my favorite, velvet brown. The iconic flower of love could be found in every state of its life cycle—tender green shoots with tiny green thorns that looked like baby teeth, buds determined not to reveal themselves any sooner than necessary, fresh blooms that resemble sleepers just opening their eyes, and full blossoms with the open-handed beauty of an old person's wrinkled face.

Such places were a far cry from my family's small vegetable garden in our backyard in Charleston, West Virginia, or my grandmother's small rose trellis anchoring the flower bed where purple pansies and pink impatiens lined up like toy soldiers at attention, but no more magnificent or well tended. I can remember my grandmother on her hands and knees talking to each flower as if it were her child, her hands caked with reddish brown soil, and her hoe nearby to dig up any weed that might dare violate the beauty of her endeavor.

Similarly, my mother and father—and eventually my siblings and I—were also as meticulous in weeding out any stray green shoot or brown stalk that attempted to drain precious water and nutrients away from our tomatoes, squash, greens, and cucumbers. I learned at an early age that weeds were not only eyesores but they were thieves, robbing the resources and deliberate attention invested in the garden's intended inhabitants. It took me until adulthood to realize that weeds of unforgiveness were far more deadly.

Gardening Tools

Scripture describes our unwillingness to forgive as a stubborn weed of bitterness that takes root in the soil of our soul and robs us of the fruits of the Spirit we are intended to produce. Moses told the Children of Israel, "Make sure there is no man or woman, clan or tribe among you today whose heart turns away from the LORD our God to go and worship the gods of those nations; make sure there is no root among you that produces such bitter poison" (Deuteronomy 29:18, NIV). The author of Hebrews writes, "See to it that no one misses the grace of God and that no bitter root grows up to cause trouble and defile many" (Hebrews 12:15, NIV). In biblical times, roots were often used for medicinal as well as culinary purposes, but it's clear in both of these descriptions that these roots are not merely a nuisance; they are deadly poison.

We have looked at the way our long-held grudges, accumulated disappointments, and secret resentments can create an enormous barrier to forgiveness as well as a huge drain on our energy and productivity. But the lesson I learned from my family's garden as I was growing up is that the best gardeners tolerate no weeds. Farmers do not wait until their entire crop is compromised or their harvest jeopardized to begin eradicating their fields of deadly weeds. They spray pesticide and use various tools to maintain their precious crops on a daily basis.

Similarly, we must tend our hearts daily to ensure that no stray comment or silent stare is allowed to embed itself beneath the surface of our thin skin. It only takes one weed left unchecked to ruin the entire agricultural system for the healthy plants that we want to grow there. One secret jealousy or offhanded remark, one unspoken conversation or one sentence said in haste, one forgotten anniversary or overlooked birthday. Whether a minuscule slight or an offense of egregious magnitude, the seeds for weeds of bitterness are the same. They all want to take root in your heart and choke you with the acrid poison of their deadly fruit—hatred, selfishness, revenge, and violence.

However, we have been given a variety of gardening tools to assist us in the process of nurturing our spiritual soil. The first one is simply a small shovel or gardening trowel that we use to uncover and identify the offense threatening to smother the tender roots of our more delicate plants such as trust and self-worth. I continue to be amazed at the people who believe that self-control and denial are synonymous or even remotely related. So many injured men and wounded women work hard to ignore the impact that has caused their impairment. It's as if someone who had survived being in the Twin Towers on 9/11 pooh-poohed their injuries and said, "What—this little scratch? Just a little mishap on the job. I'll be fine."

As we continue to see so many of our men and women in the armed services come to terms with post-traumatic stress disorder, doctors and counselors are learning that the very trait that often serves them well on the battlefield—their ability to overlook their own pain, trauma, and terror and focus on their responsibilities—also becomes a debilitating barrier to their healing and restoration once the battle is over and they have returned home to their families. The first step is often simply acknowledging that the horrors they have witnessed were indeed hellishly unfathomable and inhumane.

The atrocities witnessed and injuries—to body, mind, and soul—must be respected by attempting to give voice to their ineffable impact. Speaking about what happened tends to open the doorway and allow grief to wash through. Frequently, we are so afraid of the memories, the painful, immeasurable weight of our burdens, that we try to lock and bar the door of our souls to such grief. It feels like the grief will drown us, smother us, choke us with its unspeakable immensity. But in fact grief can be like an antiseptic that cleanses and purifies the contamination that has infiltrated the depths of our hearts.

Allowing ourselves to grieve can also be like weed killer that goes to the root of the problem. Many times we think we have dealt with our immediate emotional response at the time of an offense and don't examine ourselves to see the invisible injuries below the surface. We pick the weed and because most of it came off in our hand, we think that we have exterminated it when in fact we have only left it embedded in the most vulnerable part of our psyche.

So take your reaction to an offense as an invitation to get to the root of the problem, literally, by examining why it has hurt, wounded, or upset you. Do you feel disrespected? Dismissed? Devalued or dissed? A person can experience indigestion as well as cardiac arrest with similar symptoms; the difference is knowing how to look below the symptomatic expression of your wound and get to the real heart of the matter.

Holding on to our anger does not restore what we have lost or compensate us for our injury. Many people feel that anger is all they have left. They think, "Well, my son is dead and gone because of some drunk driver!" or "My spouse has left me for someone else" or "I've lost my retirement account just as I turned sixty-five!" Anger held is not love replaced. The reality is that love is stronger than death. Love doesn't end when caskets close or even when marriages are dissolved. You have the huge blessing of having known someone worth loving! Many people never experience the richness of a relationship in which love is given and received. If anger is all you have left, then the joy robbers win twice—they take your present peace as well as the rich memories of having had someone love you, care about you, learn with you. Just because a flower has bloomed and withered away does not mean you must plant a weed to have something in its place.

The Seat of Judgment

How we handle, acknowledge, name, and grieve our offenses is certainly the predominant kind of weeding we need to do. And yet, a second kind of insidious weed often takes root and can be even more stubborn and deadly than its botanical cousin. Surprising in origin, this bitter root is one that we cultivate ourselves. In effect, it's as if we discover a nasty weed growing in the soil of our soul and instead of digging up its roots and removing it, we water it, feed it, and treat it like a prized rosebush!

It almost seems as if we cannot bear the discovery, the possibility, of such an ugly and dangerous weed inside of us so we refuse to call it what it is and work hard instead to cultivate it. Just as Shakespeare told us that a rose by any other name would smell just as sweet, so a weed by any other name remains just as bitter! Simply put, the problem is that we refuse to forgive ourselves.

Or let's consider a different way to describe the problem, one that you might relate to easier if you are not a gardener or don't happen to have a green thumb. My guess is that most of us experienced some kind of physical punishment when we were growing up. Now, I know that corporal punishment is a bit controversial today, but when I was growing up, it was the norm. A conspiracy seemed to exist between our teachers and our parents that made escaping the consequences of our misbehavior a futile endeavor.

Looking back, I think Homeland Security could benefit from having a few of those old-fashioned mothers from my neighborhood on their team. These ladies had a unique ability to be everywhere and see everything with a surveillance system that ranged from their ultrasensitive intuition to the rotary phone connection by which my teachers would call home with classified information (or should I say, class-I-fumbled!) long before my bus got there.

If you were like me, by the time you walked in the door, you didn't even get a chance to spin the intricate story you concocted to explain your misdeed, or at the very least entertain your parents with a diversion from discussing it. On occasion, my parents would afford me the luxury of choosing my own switch. This was a crafty ploy at double punishment because if you came up short, they would pick a branch so frighteningly large that you needed a chain saw to bring it home! In spite of the psychological trauma of shopping for a switch to punish yourself, it was a highly effective way to add insult to injury!

But once the punishment was applied liberally to the seat of judgment, the storm passed rather quickly. No further acts of contrition were required other than a healthy set of sniffles, a few gasping tears with an occasional shortness of breath for theatrical value, and an extremely repentant face to match a rather sore rear end. What our parents did not do was ask us to spank ourselves. And to keep on spanking ourselves. Over and over again on a daily basis, sometimes several times a day.

We are by nature inclined to self-preservation and do not typically enjoy inflicting ourselves with pain. Instinctively we seek redemption for ourselves as opposed to retribution against ourselves. This is true for most of us with the exception of those who have so violated their own core values that they live in a perpetual state of self-flagellation. They may punish themselves subconsciously by sabotaging opportunities, cultivating eating disorders, feeling unlovable for secrets kept and consequently pushing others away, cutting themselves, drinking away the pain, over-medicating, as well as countless other self-inflicted punishments. Why would anyone deny himself or herself happiness or success, you say?

They have not dropped the charges against themselves. These

are people who cannot seem to give themselves permission to be happy or positive because secretly they are running through the woods trying to find a switch for their own punishment. It doesn't matter who else forgave them. They violated their own core values. And simply cannot forgive themselves.

Self-Afflicted

Often these people never find it in their heart to forgive themselves. Some may be great at forgiving others. They may even be so forgiving that other people who see their dysfunction as an opportunity are constantly using them. I have counseled many people who only attract the users and abusers who always justify their actions and insist that their victim deserves no better. Since the abused person agrees with this assessment and doesn't feel deserving of a better life and love, they remain in the injurious environment. In some cases these people are serving a sentence of self-loathing, and anyone who uses them is secretly the new warden from which they cannot be freed because they feel that they deserve the punishment even though they got someone else to be the switch!

Still others are very judgmental and critical of all around them to hide the seething anger they harbor against themselves. They are the people who take everyone through the same hell in which they secretly imprison themselves. You know, the kind of people who act as though they are the sole center of the universe and determine that if they aren't happy then no one else will be, either. You have heard of domestic violence. In many cases these wife-beaters (or sometimes husband beaters) have acted out on the spouse the contempt they hold against themselves. They will say things like, "Why do you make me do this? You are the reason

I am this way!" Such sick abusers want to blame the companion but deep down they are talking to themselves.

Many of the physical, emotional, or sexual abusers fall into this category. They beat the spouse as an act of violence against themselves. Now, some may not beat the spouse or abuse the children, but most save the real rage for themselves. Why? It is because they don't like themselves. The Bible says to love your neighbor as you love yourself, and it is an impossibility for them to do this while they hold themselves in such disdain.

At the core they are just self-beaters who allowed someone else to get the licks they want to give themselves. Their actions at some point in their lives have so betrayed their core values that they find themselves guilty and ashamed. They live like a dog chasing its tail, unable to break the cycle of pain they create for themselves or toward others. If it were someone else's rule they had broken they could question the validity of the rule. But when it is in fact your mistake against your own rule, you punish yourself for betraying your own code of ethics.

Core Values

Now, this issue of core values needs to be clarified for it is indeed the soil in which we cultivate so many of the weeds and the wonders of our existence. Normally when I hear anything about core values, I would categorize them as moral values, or for Christians, the biblical, scriptural standards by which we attempt to live. Now, while our core values may have been adopted in whole or in part by our early-childhood training and exposure to cultural morals, most of us have branded a unique hybrid version of values resulting from our own integration of personal priorities and public responsibilities. One doesn't have to be a moral person to have some values to which you ascribe a measurement of what you would and would not do. Your core values might be honesty or loyalty reserved for a particular group.

Often these core values are unspoken but are very real to us. Men often have what is called the "old boys' code" or women may have certain rules about how they interact in certain settings or how they can appropriately befriend, converse, or interact with someone else's husband. Teens and young adults have unspoken codes for what is considered cool, acceptable, admirable, and worthy of emulation. These rules may not be written but they are real nonetheless.

Others may value integrity in business or fidelity with a spouse. Some core values may be family-oriented rules whereby they hold high esteem for relatives, extending them a place to stay or whatever they need, though later that night they might run a mafia! Can't say they are moral people, but they do have a code of ethics, no matter how warped it may seem to others, through which they live their lives. They are committed to family if no one else.

There is an old saying that there is honor among thieves—though they break laws and commit sins there are some things that they do not do. I have known prostitutes who say they will sell their bodies but they won't kiss on a date. I know that sounds odd but I think these values give them some standard by which they can say that there is something that they will not do. It helps us to know who we are at the core of our being, the solid ground beneath the many roles we play that can experience erosion and change with the seasons. If you haven't identified your core values, it can leave you susceptible to waiting on weeds to bloom while you search for a larger switch with which to spank yourself.

Self-Respect

Your core values are the things that give you a sense of self-respect and pride. Your ability to live up to them often has a lot to do with how you see yourself. They also become the standard by which you will or will not keep friends near you. They must live up to or at least respect these values or risk being excommunicated from your circle, as these are the guiding principles by which you live your life. One of mine is loyalty and another one is a strong commitment to unconditional love among family.

Several years ago, I did an interview with a journalist who approached me with a question that was phrased, "Out of all your accomplishments, world travels, Grammy Awards, what are you the most proud of?" I thought on it a moment or two and responded, "I took care of my mother till she died." I could tell the answer seemed odd to her. But for me loyalty to someone who needed you is a very important quality! It might not earn you a brass trophy but it is one of the ways I evaluate character and integrity. I could tell that the interviewer was taken aback by my response. But my values are based on my experiences and I, like most people, give to others what I want myself.

I have a terrible disdain for disloyal behavior. To me the violation of loyalty to a friend is so hideous that it makes me angry to watch even when I am not the friend whose trust is being violated. Further, my homemade, self-created description of family centers around unconditional love and a safe place for those who may not have anywhere else to go. Now, I am not asking you to adopt my values but am just using them as an example so you can identify your own areas to which you are the most passionate. If you can list them you might be able to better understand why you do or do not have self-respect. For, my friend, self-respect is at least in part a reflection of how things are going inside of us in regard to how well we live up to our own rules.

Another reason to consider examining your core values is to help you know what stimulates and satisfies you as well as what offends and debilitates your soul. Many times we do not clarify our values to those around us. When they violate our values, we execute them with no trial or jury when they never even knew it was a rule in the first place. Have you ever lost a friend and couldn't for the life of you figure out why? Often these core values conflict in relationships and the rest is history! But is it fair? Not always. You see, it would be comparable to the state issuing a speeding ticket on a highway where there is no sign! A bit unfair, isn't it? Yet we do that all the time with people who violate what we didn't enunciate.

But as it is with most rules, sooner or later those who write them also break them! Every day we see politicians, preachers, parents, and a long list of others who violate the rules they espouse. Though these people get the press attention, in reality all of us have at times not lived up to our own standards and ideals. It is one level of conflict when you violate Senate rules or biblical rules. These may be rules that you were called on to espouse but may not always be a true reflection of your real core values. But when one really does have core values and violates those rules the anguish is far more intense.

And that is where the dilemma begins. What do you do when you have not lived up to the ideals that you deem most important? How do you look yourself in the mirror when you have violated a self-imposed standard and have no real excuse that resonates when you meditate on the mistakes you made? As conflicted as a child searching for a switch, we find ourselves often unable to forgive ourselves while at the same time trying desperately to free ourselves from the internal guilt and shame of breaking a covenant we wrote.

To the Rescue

Several years ago, I met a very gifted young man. We had so many things in common and it wasn't long before a friendship ensued. This friend was very intelligent and gifted. He could've easily written his own ticket in life as he seemingly had all the strengths that were necessary to achieve any goal he set his mind to. At the particular time I met him, he was about to explode with his business initiatives, teeming with bright ideas, and on the cusp of building an empire that was very impressive indeed. A sharp-dressing, vivacious, and charismatic individual who had the gift of gab and was well received in the upper echelon of our city.

You can well imagine why I was shocked when little by little I watched his business, family, and overall life disintegrate before my eyes. So I put on my cape and boots and decided to fire up the proverbial Batmobile and rescue him. Little did I know that you can't rescue someone who doesn't want to be rescued. I tried countless ways to support my friend (I told you loyalty is a big thing for me) over and over again. I offered contacts for business, helped with a few bills as he was short of cash, and kept looking for the cloud density over his life to lighten and dissipate.

Well, it didn't and I couldn't figure out why. I later learned as our friendship grew that he carried horrible guilt over a very complicated and pain-filled childhood. That being said, he shared a story about saying some very disrespectful things to his father. Statements said out of rage and frustration but were very damaging. He had no way of knowing that his father would be killed before he could apologize. How could he have known that his tan-

trum would be the last time they would communicate? Now with
the echo of his own words running over and over in his head, the
only one who could help him resolve his shame, he thought, was
dead.

I pointed out how a real father knows his son. I tried to explain
that though your children's words may be hurtful inevitably you
know their hearts even beyond their actions. And though he nod-
ded affirmatively and tried to absorb what I said, I knew that I was
only interrupting a self-beating that would continue when I left
the room! It was such a waste of life and painful to watch someone who had so much to give to others give nothing to himself. A
closer look at his friends and business and I saw all the signs of a
self-beater.

He gave far too much away to others. He reserved nothing
for himself. Anyone who knows business at all knows that you
can't be a baker and give away the cake, only to be left to run the
business of the crumbs. But in essence that is what my friend had
done. He was very loving but if you crossed him forgiveness wasn't
even in his vocabulary. We made some progress gradually because
he did recognize that he was his own worst enemy. He in reflection
understood that he was punishing himself and I almost begged
him to get some counseling. But sometimes our pride won't let us
cry for help even when it's our house on fire!

I was drowning in my loyalty compulsion while my friend was
distracted from communicating by his incessant need to keep the
whipping going. Sadly, the relationship tanked and as far as I know
the self-beatings continue even to this day. If only my friend would
have moved from incarcerating himself to rehabilitating himself
the story would have ended differently. It is true that at some time
or other all of us will let even ourselves down. But it isn't true that

you have to serve a life sentence in a septic tank just because you made poor judgments in the past.

Whether you're weeding out the old issues that have taken root or trying to nurture rather than neutralize your own productivity, I offer you three very basic steps that may help you to overcome the beatings and maximize the gift that God has given you called life.

1. *Admit it.*

Hiding the truth from yourself and others close to you only delays healing. While it may not be practical to shout from the rooftops every type of transgression, it is still true that this cancerous unforgiveness gathers power in secrecy. Being able to at some level reckon with the past by admitting the mistake is important. Failure to acknowledge wrongdoings is often a sign that rehabilitation isn't working. As long as we blame others for what secretly we know we caused, we cannot move forward. Many times people who hurt the most are very silent about what hurts them. They may be the life of the party for others, but that doesn't mean that they are happy inside of themselves.

I am a great believer in drawing from the bank of close friends and being able to show them not only your accomplishments but also your failures. To live your life hiding your flaws from those you love is to deny them the strength of love that builds a bond unbreakable. It keeps the relationship watered down to such a weak level that most really important relationships will not withstand the lack of trust that is exhibited when we never trust anyone with our whole self and only share with them who we wish we were.

This irreconcilable difference between who we would like to be and who we are will often bankrupt even the most sincere relationships, as we never bring our real selves with the vulnerability to the table. So people never get to love who we are, they are forced to love only our ideal self, the one we would like to be but are not.

Admitting flaws and experiencing love from people who know us helps us to love ourselves. Understand that love from them will seem awkward and may even be repulsive as it is hard to receive a love that you don't feel you warrant. But admit that, too, ask for patience, ventilate the struggle to receive love, and work on it together with people who love you enough to help free you from your dungeon.

2. *Convert it.*

Take the energy that is being spent in suffering and recycle it to use your pain to empower others. Write about it, teach about it, share your story with people who may be tempted to make the mistakes you have made and show them how you are overcoming it by using the experience that was so bad for something good. Converting our agony to motivation is a very important step in self-recovery. An explosion never occurs when energy is converted to a purpose.

If you believe as I do that everything happens for a reason, you must find that reason and turn those experiences that threaten to detonate in your life into a useful energy source that empowers you and others.

In church we say that our ministry is often made from our misery. While on the surface that may sound strange, in reality it is the power of conversion that makes us able to use our pain for power to help others through a storm. Now, I can imagine that some things that cause us not to be able to forgive ourselves may be too personal or painful to share in a public forum. But finding some way to give meaning to your malady is important even if it isn't the sort of thing you can readily discuss. Helping others prevent or avoid similar pain is often a healing balm. You can't compensate for what you have lost, but you can contribute to the well-being of others.

3. *Close it.*

There has to be a moment where you say, I am through paying the price for my sins. I recognize that this destructive way of coping neither reverses what I have done nor does it benefit anyone, including me. I am going to close the door on the destructive behavior my pain creates and close this cycle before it destroys me. Closure may involve having long-overdue conversations, writing letters to ask for someone else's forgiveness, or serving others without telling them why you are motivated to give them your time and talents.

In this life we will never know the perfect beauty of the Garden of Eden. But we can know what it's like to weed out the bitter roots that threaten our peace and well-being. We can let go of the blame we place on ourselves and move to a new place of freedom and fruit-bearing productivity.

thirteen
Physician, Heal Thyself

One of the most devastating challenges of any catastrophe emerges when your need is greatest and yet the capacity for assistance is at its lowest. We witnessed such a devastating collision in 2010 during the seven-point earthquake in Haiti, when the shuddering convulsions of the earth reduced entire cities, villages, and neighborhoods to rubble. As office buildings, hotels, and businesses toppled over like a child's building blocks, thousands and thousands of lives were lost and over a million more people found themselves wounded and homeless.

Certainly one of the most frustrating aspects of this nightmare emerged when those in need of critical care realized that virtually all the hospitals, clinics, and medical facilities were also destroyed by the calamity. As joyous a discovery as it was to uncover survivors beneath the layers of dust and debris, it was all the more frustrating to realize that there was no place to take them for emergency medical attention. At the time when these afflicted people needed expert assistance the most, the same disaster that wounded them with such a debilitating blow also claimed their sources of recovery.

We witness similar compounded catastrophes anytime a hurricane, tornado, or tsunami leaves a wake of collateral damage behind its front wave of physical ferocity. The injured, wounded, and dying initially have no place to find emergency treatment or medical attention. In my experiences and encounters with emotionally wounded individuals, I have discovered a deeply troubling parallel.

Men and women suffering from the emotional devastation of betrayal, addiction, and other crises often turn to their local church to find acceptance, encouragement, and spiritual support they know they need to facilitate their recovery. However, these wounded individuals often discover that the church members' response in their time of need only exacerbates the problem. Instead of acceptance, they find subtle exclusivity and a hypocritical hierarchy of self-righteousness. Rather than receiving encouragement, these wounded souls feel the sting of icy stares and whispered gossip behind the exclamation of "God bless you, brother!" There is no spiritual life support, only the slow, torturous drip of an insidious IV of annihilation.

My fear is that the Christian church, which should be a spiritual hospital providing soul care, has instead become a dangerous battle zone of pretension, prejudice, conformity, and exclusion. If we are to find lasting freedom and spiritual healing on our journey of forgiveness, then we must reclaim the church as a community of God's people, forgiven by his mercy and grace, caring for others in need.

Shooting the Wounded

Imagine that you have a good friend who is very ill and calls you up one day and asks for your best advice. Suffering from multiple injuries as well as a critical disease, she asks you to recommend a good place for medical treatment, a place where she can receive the dedicated attention and intensive intervention she needs in order to have her health restored. Without even having to reflect on her request, you enthusiastically share with her the name and location of your own clinic and mention several of the doctors and medical staff by name. With abiding gratitude, your friend thanks you and says that she will go there right away.

Several weeks pass before you see your friend, and when you run into her in your local Starbucks, she appears to be doing quite well. Her clothes are beautifully coordinated, she is immaculately groomed, her hair perfectly coiffed, and her demeanor pleasantly polite. As the two of you converse over your lattes, you inquire about the status of her health and her treatment at the clinic you recommended. Hesitant at first, she begins to choose her words carefully, clearly becoming more and more reticent to discuss her prognosis in great detail.

Scrutinizing your friend, looking into the listless, wistful center of her eyes, you realize that she remains quite sick. Beneath the veneer of her flawless makeup, you see sallow skin with burst blood vessels and more wrinkles than a linen skirt packed in a suitcase. In fact, you realize that she's sicker now than she was the last time you saw her!

No, I am not summarizing an old episode of *The Twilight Zone* or the plot for some new big-screen sequel to *The Stepford Wives*. Every week, millions of people visit such places and, like your friend mentioned above, never receive actual treatment or the medication they so desperately need to restore their physical, emotional, and spiritual health. Instead they are coached on how to cover up their wounds, ignore their internal injuries, disguise their scars, and camouflage their condition.

The philosophy of this place seems to be that if you pretend the painful dis-ease of your actual condition is not a problem, then it will cease to be one. Basically, both the spoken and subtly implicit rules of the place dictate maintaining a façade of perfect health and well-being. You must act healthy no matter how sick you may know you really are, and the last thing you are permitted to do is discuss your condition with anyone, whether another patient or an outside observer. All the while, countless men and women of all ages, races, and socioeconomic levels remain desperate to have their health restored but are denied such care in the very place where it should be the only priority.

Similarly, this place also kills its own kind whenever they fall outside of the socially and culturally prescribed code of conduct befitting medical professionals at such a renowned, reputable institution. Instead of being the first to receive treatment so that they could then in kind serve and administer aid to patients with similar needs, these medical professionals are deemed unfit and quietly whisked away and buried beneath a layer of preposterous posturing and pretentious power.

This is not what anyone wants this place called church to be, especially those of us who have spent our lives serving, building, and growing its resources. No, we long for it to be a hospital for wounded souls, a critical-care clinic where people who have made mistakes can find second chances, and a place of jubilant celebration where prodigals are welcomed home. Scripture tells us the church is the Bride of Christ, the Communion of Saints, and the fellowship of those who know and love the Lord. As a community of Christians, the church is exhorted to be a bright and illuminative beacon into the dark recesses of our painfully shadowed world, a home for repentant sinners, and a shelter for those who seek to know the truth.

Tragically enough, in many communities, the church has lost its bearings and has not retained its commitment to biblical principles and Godly compassion. My worst fear is that it has become the source of an epidemic of prejudice, judgmental attitudes, and hypocrisy. A country-club caricature of itself, it often seems like one more place where elitism rules and those with the right clothes, best cars, and most money come to mingle with their own kind. Ministry projects become tokenlike displays of the institution's philanthropic power and self-congratulatory attempts to reach down with a few crumbs for the many less fortunate beneath them.

What I hear from so many people, especially those I encounter who tell me they want no part of any faith-based institution, is that the church today has become a place where the disease of hypocrisy runs rampant, where an epidemic of denial pulls a tight curtain of performance-based propriety around the many patients who are told about the healing power of Christ but rarely see it. Ministry leaders prescribe one medicine and take another and when their own improprieties come to the surface, then they are removed from the pulpit like a malignant tumor being extricated from the body.

Tragically, the wounded are welcomed but then shot if they do not pretend to get better based on their own performance. No one discusses the clandestine affairs and dirty secrets of the human hearts involved. The same addictions, marital problems, infidelities, gossiping, lying, cheating, stealing, and betrayals exist here as in any other human community. Only here they cannot be talked about except in the way that one describes a group of people suffering from some rare disease in another part of the world.

I don't know about you, but when I hear such descriptions and the data that lead individuals to such harsh conclusions, I feel a huge burden of responsibility, both as a Christian as well as clergy, to reverse such damage and restore the Bride of Christ to her intended beauty as a place of healing, acceptance, and life-giving balm. My faith in God and in the church as his instrument of peace, his hand of healing, and his conduit of love into a broken world remains unchecked. But we must make some changes if this physician is indeed going to heal itself in a way that restores others to life.

Back to Church

Perhaps you have only had positive, life-building, faith-growing experiences with the church and do not understand the harsh descriptions and uncharitable language that I have relayed here. If this is the case, then I praise God with you and rejoice with thanksgiving and only ask that you display the same spirit of generosity and compassion to those you encounter. You have much to teach the rest of us even as you continue to inspire us with your hope and ongoing faith in God's ability to use the church as his hands, his feet, his eyes, and ears.

Or maybe your reaction to this issue stirs up old wounds to the point that you do not think that what I have mentioned is critical enough. You may have experienced a deep and painful rejection and disenfranchisement from the very place where you had pinned your last hopes for finding help. Perhaps you encountered the unfathomable spiritual abuse of a church with corrupt leadership, fleecing the very flock it was supposed to be nurturing and protecting.

You may have given up on the church and found that the one place that should be like the electric utility company in your community—a conduit of power and illumination—has instead become the weekly sanitation service, hauling its garbage to the curb. You may believe that the church and its members have brought such a negative and shameful reputation on themselves by their sanctimonious subterfuge and self-righteous indignity.

Regardless of on which end of the spectrum you find yourself, I believe most of us would agree on two very apparent conclusions. First, the church should be a place of healing and restoration, a bright reflection of the mercy, grace, and love of our Father God. He is the One who welcomed his wayward son with open arms after the child had embarrassed himself and his family. He remains the One who welcomes us back home again and again. As we have seen in prior chapters, if we have not received the grace he gives to us so freely, then we are impaired in our ability to extend grace to our own offenders.

Second, at present the church is not fulfilling this charge honorably or effectively. In fact, based on the many people I counsel and converse with about their past church experiences, I'm afraid the church has become a barrier to the process of forgiveness and not the conduit of grace it was created to be. If we are to experience the joy, freedom, and renewal that come with practicing the art of forgiveness in our lives, then we must reclaim the church as a center for healing spiritual sickness rather than the germ-carrying instrument of more disease.

I believe the problems in the Christian church here in the first rays of our twenty-first-century dawn emerge from the convergence of three areas—church leadership, church membership, and the church's relationship to the world at large. These issues are both within and without, running from the pulpit to the prayer meeting and back again, burdening all of us with a holy mandate to reverse the damage and try and resuscitate this most precious patient who often appears to be gasping for her last breaths.

Church Leadership

The first problem is one of church leadership. There is an insidious cycle that creates an impenetrable loop of leaders being held on pedestals that seem to go higher and higher the more successful the appearance of the particular church. Because God's holy perfection and inherent goodness often feel abstract and intangible, people look to clergy for glimpses of the divine in action, a more than reasonable expectation, as well as an understandable responsibility of those in church leadership.

Part of the problem then emerges when the congregation loses sight of the humanity of its leaders. They want someone to both model a flawless Christian life as well as enforce it within the walls of the church. Over the course of my thirty-five years in ministry, I have often been amused at the response of people from my church when they encounter me in the neighborhood at the grocery store, or the dry cleaner's, the dentist's office, or the drive-thru at McDonald's. They often seemed shocked to realize that I am just like them in terms of needing the same gallon of milk, pressed suit, or Big Mac and fries that they do! They don't consider that I participate, just as we all do, in the everyday routines and mundane activities that are part of life. Taken out of the context of our usual encounters centered on our relationship at church, it's startling for people to see me picking out breakfast cereal or paying a parking ticket just like everyone else.

It reminds me of being a kid and running into one of my grade-school teachers in the produce aisle of our local grocery store back in Charleston, West Virginia, where I grew up. Walking alongside my mother as she pushed our cart, I stopped dead in my tracks when suddenly there in front of me was Mrs. Simpson, my fourth-grade math teacher, squeezing a cantaloupe! It was like seeing an alien suddenly land in our midst and nonchalantly begin to do the weekly shopping. It was one of those moments when I realized that the context in which we know someone is only one of the facets of their humanity and one dimension of their personality focused and filtered through their role in the community. For all I know, Mrs. Simpson may have been just as shocked to know that I could behave myself long enough to pick out a box of Corn Flakes!

Please realize that in elevating clergy to superhuman status, church members also play on the very real human weaknesses within every man or woman. Namely, that little, three-letter, dirty word, E-G-O. Depending on the personality and character deficiencies within someone, the last thing they may need is to be told how holy, perfect, and religious they are. An inherent performance-based standard within such a person becomes fueled by such attention and adoration, inflating their self-worth to the point where they either go into denial and self-delusion over their own shortcomings and moral failures or else they compartmentalize them into a hidden, secret part of themselves that no one must ever discover.

Then when their transgression is discovered or exposed, or when they confess because the weight of their burden has compressed their emotional spine to the point of threatening their life and sanity, these clergy experience the congregation's contempt for violating the illusion of performance perfection. Church action may be brutal, swift, and silent with no one talking about the pastor, his problem, or his unexplained sudden absence, or it may attempt to be more gracious under the guise of a "restoration plan" with an "accountability team" and a paid leave of absence from his or her responsibilities. In either case, the effect is typically the same. The pastoral leader is treated as a pariah, forced into exile, and left to face his shame, pain, and resentment alone.

There's a story, which may be apocryphal, told about the renowned African-American surgeon Dr. Charles R. Drew, who lived and practiced during the first half of the twentieth century. Dr. Drew pioneered our modern methods of blood transfusions and innovated the storage and utilization of blood and plasma in what we now call blood banks. Through his professional insight and administrative foresight, he was responsible for saving countless lives during World War II. Thousands of wounded soldiers received emergency transfusions from blood banks that Dr. Drew helped establish and implement.

Later, after the war, Dr. Drew was driving to a medical conference in Tuskegee when he lost control of his vehicle and crashed. Rushed to the nearest hospital, along with his passengers, Dr. Drew did not receive adequate treatment to save his life. While it has been disputed, many people have speculated that he was not treated promptly because of his race. In effect, Dr. Drew was denied the blood transfusion—which he himself developed—that would have saved his life.

I can't think of a more powerful or revealing picture of how our clergy are treated today. Instead of allowing our spiritual leaders to be martyred for being human like the rest of us, consider how powerful it would be for them to receive the mercy, grace, and healing love of those they have served so faithfully up until that point. If we are willing to see our clergy as wounded healers rather than superheroes, we have taken the first step in changing the artery blockage threatening the heart of the church.

Problems in the Pew

The second area that must be addressed if the church is to return to being a conduit of forgiveness deals with church membership. This issue has many variables and several layers as well, but for our discussion, I would like to focus on one of them—expectations. We have already looked at the problem with having unyielding expectations of church clergy, but the same preconceived notions of perfection are often held and used against people alongside one another in the pew.

Virtually every church I have ever visited or know of stresses the importance of community. Whether it's through adult education, what we typically think of as "Sunday school," small groups that meet in people's homes during the week, a ladies' prayer circle, or a men's Bible study, churches want their members interacting, relating, connecting. This is indeed one of the most wonderful benefits that church can offer—a sense of having a spiritual home, a place to belong, a family who loves and supports you.

However, when the problem of unforgiveness festers and multiplies within the walls of a church, the resulting pandemic stunts spiritual growth in record proportions. It might be a problem with gossip and spreading rumors, feeding our individual prurient imaginations with lurid details that may have no basis in fact but merely stem from someone's own repressed desires and secret fantasies. It could be a competitive game of one-upmanship in which certain individuals consider themselves more spiritual than the rest because of their hours spent in prayer, Bible study, the deacons' committee, and worship team meetings. Or it may be as basic as self-righteousness expressed through judgmental attitudes and treatment of others, a problem Jesus frequently encountered in his day.

In fact, he told a parable before a group that included many of the "perfect" religious leaders, the Pharisees, of that time. Jesus said that two men went to church, each wanting to pray before God. One of them, a proper Pharisee, came down to the altar front and center and prayed out loud, "God, I thank you that I am not like other people—robbers, evildoers, adulterers—or even like this tax collector. I fast twice a week and give a tenth of all I get" (Luke 18:11-12, NIV). You know the type—they lower their voice into this deep, James Earl Jones kind of tone and then drone on and on in a way that makes them look spiritually superior to the rest of us.

In sharp contrast, the other man, the tax collector, a profession despised then about as much as an IRS auditor might be today, kept his distance from the altar with his head bowed. Beating his breast as a sign of humble contrition, the tax man simply prayed, "God, have mercy on me, a sinner" (Luke 18:13, NIV). Just in case anyone listening missed his point, Jesus made it very clear, "I tell you that this man, rather than the other, went home justified before God. For all those who exalt themselves will be humbled, and those who humble themselves will be exalted" (Luke 18:14, NIV). God clearly loves those who know they need him and appreciates it when we remember this not only before him but in our encounters with others as well. None of us is worthy before him. The prophet Isaiah said that our best actions are nothing but filthy rags compared to the holiness of God.

If we are to correct the wayward course of the church, then we as Christians must treat one another as fellow sinners who all need the gift of God's grace as much as the porn addict, the rapist, the embezzler, or the adulterer. None of us is any better than anyone else in God's eyes—or any worse. It's been said that God is no respecter of persons, meaning that he does not play favorites with his children and esteem the rich, the good looking, the proper and polite. Based on what we know of Jesus's interactions, it seems that if he had a preference about who he hung out with, then it was most likely people society marginalized and dismissed—such as the tax collectors, the prostitutes, uneducated fishermen, the blind and the lame, the lepers.

We must risk being appropriately transparent with one another, sharing our ongoing struggles as well as our victories. We must ask for help when we need it and we must give it freely and without judgment when others in the church community ask it from us. If we are to remove the dark tarnish of unforgiveness from our churches, then we must use collaboration, cooperation, and concentration as our silver polish. Battling the injuries of life and the sickness of sin, we are all patients here, helping one another experience the same healing that we ourselves receive.

Public Face

The third major minefield in our church today stems from the way we relate to the world and our culture around us. Instead of relating to people outside the church with servant leadership and divine love, the church has become known today for the products it pickets, the movies it boycotts, and the people it condemns. Now, I am certainly not asserting that the church should not take a stand for what is right in the depravity and dysfunction of our dark world. The problem as I see it is that we have made negation our priority. The church has become known for what it is against instead of what it is for!

Partisan politics also enter the picture, often creating rifts and divisions unnecessarily. The public face of the church has become distorted from the calm, beautiful countenance of a bride beneath her veil whispering "I love you" to that of an old, angry shrew always nagging and complaining about everything. The emphasis has shifted from relational reconciliation to public relations. Many churches seem to set themselves up as the gatekeepers to heaven, pronouncing acceptance for those who agree with them and align themselves with their causes and condemning anyone who does not.

Which brings us to the problem of exclusivity. Instead of welcoming the diversity of the culture around us, too often churches become one more homogeneous group agreeing with itself about what it believes. The good news of God's love and forgiveness is that it is for all people! In his many letters to the early Christian churches, themselves a ragtag multicultural assembly of Jews, Greeks, Romans, and Samaritans, Paul makes it clear that these demographic markers disappear within the Body of Christ. He says there is no longer a distinction between the Jew and the Gentile, between the slave and his master, even between male and female (Romans 10:12).

Instead of hate-filled blogs proclaiming who they think is going to hell, churches should be concentrating on attracting all people with the sweet fragrance of God's grace. Instead of testing political candidates on being politically correct, we need to demonstrate respect for the leaders already in office. Jesus said that people would know we are his followers not by how we separated ourselves from others who are different than we are, but by our love. If we are to practice forgiveness, then we need to show the world what real love looks like, how true healing takes place, whenever we get the chance.

Emergency Care

I pray that you have never had to make a trip to the emergency room in the middle of the night. With five children as well as having cared for aging parents, I have seen my share of after-hours hospital visits, as you can imagine. And if you have lived very long at all, then you know too well what it can be like in such a crisis-treatment facility.

In the very best ERs, there is sufficient personnel to handle the influx of patients awaiting immediate treatment, many for life-threatening injuries or terminal conditions. There are adequate facilities with the necessary equipment, clinical devices, and medications. Most of all, in the very best emergency rooms, you will find a dedicated team of compassionate men and women who love helping others, who are committed to the well-being of each and every patient that they encounter.

This is my prayer for how our churches can function—nonexclusively, for there must be aftercare and full recovery, along with restoration and training of more servant leaders. If we want to put our forgiveness into practice, then we share it with those around us, both inside and outside the church. We must be able to treat people where they are and allow God to work through us instead of blocking the path.

The Christian church has withstood centuries of unspeakable

crimes, hideous secrets, and abusive authority, both within and beyond its hallowed walls. And Christ has never abandoned his Bride but will continue to love her so that she might be robed in his righteousness and adorned with his grace, drawing all people to such holy beauty. We must reclaim it as the Body of Christ, a community of the forgiven administering compassion, healing, and grace to others in need.

fourteen
Available for What's Next

There is no need to forgive what's behind you if you aren't going to embrace what is before you. You may have absorbed every truth and utilized every tool that I've shared throughout this entire book, but now it's not just a matter of feeling lighter. It's a matter of your unique, personalized, stylized purpose from your Maker. It's about immersing yourself in the flood of fulfillment that has been blocked by the dam of past disappointments. Simply put, it's about turning your head around from looking behind you, realizing where you are right now, and then looking forward to your future. It's no accident that the word "repentance" means turning away from the dead end and returning to the open road of forgiveness.

The word "forgiving" means you have been "giving" to that which is prior, before your present moment and the gifts of your future. Now that you have been liberated from old grudges, released from deep-seated resentments, and set free from the snares of unforgiveness, a most important question looms like a huge billboard beside the highway: What will you do with yourself? To what endeavor will you give that extra energy and passion that you just freed up?

New Investments

Most of us have to live within our means. We have to live with the fact that our money is a limited resource. Most people do not have endless amounts of cash, nor do they have endless amounts of energy. Most of us must decide where we are going to put our money by prioritizing what is most important. Think of your energy the same way. Now that you are through investing in that which is behind you, free and clear of past debts, you are ready to invest in that which is before you.

Your energy is like money in that it has the power to give you something in exchange for your investment. It is also like money in that you can reallocate it and change your life by changing where you distribute the various resources you have available. It is like money because energy is only valuable when it is converted into something.

Consider the significance of money for a moment. You can't eat it, you can't drive it, and you can't wear it. But if you have it, you can exchange it for food, transportation, and clothing. The amount of money you have, in turn, largely determines the kind of food you eat, the type of car you drive, and where you buy your blue jeans. Your energy is the same way. By itself, energy is only a commodity until you expend it on something. The business of forgiveness is about re-budgeting your energy supply and attention span toward something other than what happened to you in the past.

If you are like me, you can easily spend above your budget and get off track. When you do so, you don't just throw out the entire budget for the rest of the month because you overspent one weekend. You forgive yourself and get back on track. You think about what you overspent on and why. You learn what you can in hopes of not repeating such a splurge again and move on.

Forgiveness is like this as well. Certain things may happen and distract you, drawing you back into an attitude you thought you had conquered. You may encounter past offenders who have not changed who know just how to push your buttons. Or people whom you have forgiven and with whom you have attempted to rebuild trust may disappoint you once again. When you encounter such moments, don't fall completely off the wagon and relapse into the abyss of malice and bitterness. No, instead, get back on track and remind yourself of other priorities more worthy of your thoughts, time, and attention.

Now is the time to decide where you are going to direct this attention that was being utilized to keep anger and frustration alive. It is time to birth something more worthy of your attention and time. It's time to make yourself available for the next opportunity waiting just around the corner.

Wasted Energy

Do you remember how much crude oil was spilled in the Gulf of Mexico when the *Deepwater Horizon* oil rig exploded? Not one day went by that we weren't inundated with the ecosystem being threatened by the wasteful release of thousands of gallons of oil into the sea. Every organism in any contact with the waters of the gulf, from the tiniest tadpole to the many human inhabitants along its shores, suffered the incident's life-threatening impact. Even now many scientists suggest that there will be long-term problems resulting from such a massive spill of crude contaminants.

BP, the monolithic corporation formerly known as British Petroleum, was skewered throughout our media for allowing such a waste of energy to produce the collateral damage to our beaches, wildlife, industry, and tourism. Many lost their lives. The ecosystem, barely recovered and still in a fragile state from the ravages of Katrina, languished in the devastation of millions of barrels of wasted energy hemorrhaging into it. Even as these human and natural habitats struggle to heal again, the enormous energy wasted, both in raw crude oil and in resources spent to contain and halt it, can never be recovered. In fact, experts tell us that the enormous energy wasted in ending this debacle was ultimately far more expensive than the cost of the oil excreted through the breach. And of course, it's impossible to put a price tag on the health and well-being of our irreplaceable natural resources.

Similarly, when we invest in staunching old wounds but refuse to let them heal, we are investing our resources in a futile endeavor. As we have seen, we ourselves keep the wound open through our bitterness and unwillingness to forgive and heal. Our wasted energy isn't just a sad loss of opportunity or economy. It has peripheral damage. Imagine the family devastation when Mom and Dad won't forgive. We know it costs them, but what we don't know is how their emotional spill damages their relationships with the children, and then their children's children. Dysfunction spills for generations, polluting countless individual lives, if it isn't capped in some way.

Today, though, the oil spill has been abated and the oil that was clinging to the backs of birds and causing the premature death of fish has been returned to its proper, productive, energy-giving function. Its productivity is fueling engines for transportation, providing fuel for lights and machinery to function, for heating, and so much more—all because someone capped the waste and redirected its loss to a more noble pursuit.

Forgiveness caps the leak in your own energy and enables you to stop the damage it causes you, minimize the peripheral damage it causes others, and ultimately restore to you the infusion of energy denied to your dreams by the emotionally and physically draining leak from your human soul. I challenge you to begin to plan for the new energy and efforts you have saved to be redirected to something more deserving of your time.

The "could've, would've, should've"s have been driven away and been replaced by the "I can, I will, and I shall" of it all! Your positive attitude is now lurching forward like a once-stalled car after it has been reenergized. This is the most exciting part of our journey because now we have moved past what the apostle Paul calls the process of "forgetting those things which are behind" and we are now ready to enter into the second stage of "reaching those things which are before"!

Lifting Weights

The question is, What would you do if you knew you were unstoppable? What would you go after if you had no fear? How far would you excel if the weight weren't there anymore? These questions frame the impossibilities-turned-opportunities waiting for you now that you have redirected your energy and decided to live without the constraint of so much wasted energy.

One lady with whom I shared this declaration of independence had at one time been at the brink of suicide. As she struggled to come to terms with this reallocation of her energy, I asked her in a counseling session to do an exercise. She was to write out an unrestricted vision of what she would do with the next ten years of her life if she did not have to focus on what she'd gone through in her past.

When she brought her homework to our next session, I took her vision-casting list and read it back to her and asked, "Then what's keeping you from living this out?" She stuttered a moment and said, "I didn't think I could. It's—it's too overwhelming." I responded, "You couldn't before because you were working from the deficit of an energy leak. But now, you can do something with that restored energy flow."

When we lift the weights of our pasts, it doesn't mean that there isn't another endeavor waiting for us to carry. In some ways, it's like the process of cross-training. Athletes lift weights so that they can be stronger in their particular sport. They may be runners or ballerinas, football players or basketball stars, but they realize that weight training makes them stronger and better-equipped to return to their primary focus. When we practice forgiveness, we use the muscles we have been forced to develop to return to what should have been our primary focus all along.

Too often we get so close to moving on, so close to really changing that it terrifies us. It's as if we climbed the mountain without looking down until we approached the top and now when we look down, our vertigo threatens to unnerve our resolve and send us spiraling downward. I believe the final phase of letting go of our past wounds is realizing what we have had all along and forgiving ourselves for not choosing to heal sooner.

Brotherly Love

One of my favorite stories in the Bible is Jesus's parable about the prodigal son (see Luke 15). There are three main characters in the story: two brothers and their father. The younger brother requested from his father an early gift of an inheritance that traditionally was only given posthumously.

Most of us have heard about this young man; however, we may not have realized that among the parable's many messages is one on the value of patience and waiting until you have matured enough to handle what will one day be yours. The prodigal son was so unready, so immature in making his premature request that when he got what he thought he wanted, he mismanaged what he was given.

Mismanagement of an opportunity often results when we prematurely grab the blessings around us. The wayward son spent his money on partying and promiscuity and procuring so-called friends only to end up having to lower himself and his standards until he bore no resemblance to who and what he should have been. His associations declined to a level where he was so far from his father's teachings, literally lower than a pig's belly in the mud, that he finally began to recognize his dire need. He demanded something that he could not handle, squandered it, and found himself encumbered by a much lesser life than he had imagined possible.

The moral of the prodigal's story seems crystal clear. However, many people do not notice another key player in the story, one with a lesson for us that is just as vital to our well-being. The prodigal's older brother stayed at home with his father, the dutifully responsible elder child, but secretly he resented his younger brother's relationship with their father. He had remained judicious and dependable and what had it gotten him? The elder brother never slept with harlots or wasted his inheritance from his father.

The older brother's issue, though quieter and not as audacious as his brother's, is equally dangerous. Big brother was filled with a bitter, angry spirit, feeling like he had been ignored and neglected. Consequently, when his younger brother comes home and their father throws a welcome-back barbeque like he's never seen, the older brother cannot participate. He had spent his days rehearsing his frustration and now had to miss his chance at celebration!

He felt violated by his younger brother's ingratitude and his father's extravagant generosity, never realizing his own lack of appreciation of the blessings before him. The older brother's sin isn't one of commission but one of omission. The younger brother had been gone, feared dead, and when their family reunited the older brother was enraged that his dad would throw a lavish party for someone who had been so derelict in his responsibilities and disrespectful in his sensibilities. He refused to celebrate someone whose past mistakes had been so vile.

Consequently, he stayed away from the celebration until the father came out and spoke to him. In essence, he said, "You need not long for a celebration you could've had long ago. Son, you could have had a party at any time. All that I have is yours." His father's admonition is gentle but equally sobering in its message. Basically, you spent your energy being bitter and resentful of your brother when you could've been celebrating your life the entire time! The truth is that your brother's actions didn't stop your party. Your attitude about your brother's actions stopped your party!

Perhaps in our younger years we all tend to relate to the prodigal more easily. He's young, foolish, and learns the hard way about what it means to grow up, and about what it means to be loved unconditionally. As we get older and more mature (at least, so we think!), we often shift into the older brother's mind-set. We're not all being wild and wicked, getting into trouble and overtly acting sinful. And yet we stand back and judge others who are in that phase and resent the fact that we're being so dutiful and responsible. In other words, our attitude is just as bad as the wild child's—maybe worse because often we are not being honest about it!

How many times has our attitude stopped us from maximizing our life because of the choices of someone else? This stern and loving rebuke from the elder son's father applies still today to the "could haves" of life. How many opportunities are wasted grumbling about the actions of someone else over which you have no control? One of the many messages I get from this story is the danger of missing my opportunities because I wasted my energy focusing on what someone else did.

I wonder what you "could have" done with the time and energy you poured like oil flooding into the gulf by comparing yourself to someone else? What chances were poisoned by that wasted energy? What opportunities obscured by the murky film of your bitter attitude? Perhaps this is the final area in which you need to forgive others as well as yourself.

If we are to be available for what's next, the next blessing, the next gift from God, the next amazing opportunity, then we must not compare our journey to anyone else's. We must not resent the grace and mercy showered upon someone else, holding up our self-righteous umbrella to keep us dry because we think we're so much better than they are. No, the same mercy, grace, and goodness have been ours—and continue to be ours—all along!

True Grit

Now that you have your leak fixed and your focus back, you have some planning to do. Your experience isn't a failure but a learning opportunity that should now help you to determine what is and isn't the highest and best use of your time and energy. Your life experiences should make you energy efficient! You conserve your energy from that which isn't productive so that you can spend your energy on that which is helpful in fulfilling your purpose.

In order to determine your highest and best use, you must search for clues of destiny. Your destiny is never tied to that which you lost. And it is always connected to that which remains, all the resources both internal and external that you have left in your possession. Accessing what you have is far better than wasting energy grieving over what you lost. Take inventory of your wisdom gained, experience earned, and insight gleaned. These pearls are valuable because they are born from the experiences you have accrued. They are as unique and personal as your fingerprints and belong to you in a way that no one can ever take from you.

Like an oyster that builds calcium around a grain of sand lodged in its shell, your irritations make your pearls. Once a wound, now it is wisdom that you wouldn't have otherwise. These are hard-earned pearls that you will no longer cast before swine. As you determine the worth of what you have, you also learn who is and isn't worthy of such a great investment. It cost you something to be who you are. Dive for your pearls like a treasure hunter searching the ocean floor, discovering the beautiful gift that's waiting inside the grit.

If you keep searching, there is more in you than that which you gained from the struggles you have had. There is also the value of the hidden treasure of your true identity and personal gifts. Your past struggle is a sign that you had value before you had the painful experiences. Your adversary wouldn't attack you if you had no value. I often say, seldom do you hear of a bag lady being robbed. Why? Primarily because the thief only robs people who possess something worth taking. What happened to you is a sign of what you possessed before the trouble came. You must go back and value what you have inside. None of us is born into this life without treasure buried within.

Commencement Exercise

You wouldn't use a computer to hold a door open even though it could have the weight necessary to prop open the door. You wouldn't do it because the computer would be underutilized in that role and you would rather save its energy, impact, and potential for a higher, more worthwhile use. If you understand this comparison, then please understand that you have the ability to do more than be hurt over the past and languish in the despair of your injustices. You have a higher calling, a more noble purpose. And most of all, you have a potential that should never be underutilized.

In order to arrive at a better place, you may have to change your associations and make them more congruent with your destination. You may have to sharpen raw skills to bring them to a marketable status. Or you may have to use this new energy to harness the wisdom and teach others how to avoid similar ditches in life. Any of these are a better use of your time. All of them restore life and facilitate energy rather than drain life and siphon energy away.

Perhaps instead of being distracted by who left you or betrayed you, maybe it's time to celebrate those who stood by you. Your supporters and encouragers are deserving of a celebration. Acknowl-edging them and appreciating them is important. Perhaps you should call whoever God used to nurse you and tell them you are off the critical list and are able now to navigate better than be-fore. Take them to dinner! Or have some celebration to connote the transition that has been made from the illness and injury of the past to the health and wellness of the present.

Celebrations help us mark closure of one season and invite the next one. It is so important to celebrate decisions. It is why my Jewish friends have a bar mitzvah. It is why we as Christians have a baptism. Birthdays, weddings, and new babies should all be cel-ebrated. Ceremonies of this nature often signify a rite of passage. To those who have climbed over such large emotional and spiri-tual hurdles a celebration becomes a graduation ceremony! When you have passed over a major hurdle, a celebration is appropriate.

Don't be dissuaded by the naysayers, the critics, or the hat-ers. If they don't see the value in what you've done, that doesn't diminish the price of your oil. You must now understand that those who do not celebrate your growth may be those who needed you to stay afflicted to ensure their significance in your life. Or worse still, they may be those who are jealous of your survival or improvement. Healthy people welcome your healing and support your growth!

Just as graduation celebrations are usually called commence-ment exercises—a step into the new future—I want to leave you with one final assignment. Using your freshly restored and accrued en-ergy, I want you to reinvest the commodity of your energy's power toward your new direction. Would you consider making a list, no matter how short or long it is, of your plans to move forward? A visual map or a written guide that begins with where you are now, not where you've come from, is necessary to help guide you toward where you want to go.

We have tried this in my church with amazing results. I had our church members write a vision of where they wanted to be or changes they wanted to make in the coming months. They wrote it down on December 29 and I sent it back to them in a self-addressed envelope around the month of May. I did it so that they could see how close they were toward where they wanted to be. I also did it that early in the year in case they had gotten off track. If they had slipped, they would have time to get back on course before year's end.

I thought they might forget about our little exercises, but the closer we got to the date, the more I started to get inquiries. When are you going to send us our lists? The question alone was a sign that they were yet mindful of their commitment to themselves. Maybe you would benefit from committing to remain free from the contamination of wasted energy and perhaps be further inspired by a timeline to go do something that you couldn't have done before when your energies were allocated elsewhere. I am excited about what you are about to do.

As we prepare to conclude our discussion of forgiveness and its essential life-giving power, I leave you with this thought: Whoever said that opportunity knocks only once must have died young. If you live long enough, you discover that life does give second chances—and third and fourth chances. You learn that love comes more than once to those who are open to receive it. If you live long enough, you get to see people go broke and rebound financially.

I have seen the homeless person become a homeowner after losing their first house and wondering if they'd ever have the resources to own again. I have seen divorced people fall in love again. I have lived long enough to see wayward children mature and change their perspective. I have seen the illiterate earn advanced degrees and inmates turn into interns!

You see, if you are open and available, opportunity does knock more than once. When yours does, and I know it will, open the door and scream this welcome as loud as you can, "I am available for what's next!" Now that you have your focus back, set a course to use your newly conserved energy to mine the treasure you have inside and to use it to benefit those who are worthy of its investment. Lay down what you have carried as a burden so that you can handle the blessings waiting for your embrace. Isn't it time that you accepted your destiny's invitation to dance?

Conclusion:
Multiplying Mercy

What would you say to someone who carries around a beautifully wrapped present but never opens it? If forgiveness, as we have seen, is the gift you give yourself, then I pray that you have unwrapped the present and have started using it to the fullest. From my experience as a pastor, entrepreneur, and observer of diverse peoples, I would venture that forgiveness is the most significantly underutilized aspect of adult maturation. People often believe it's important conceptually but reserve forgiveness for a few moments in a prayer at church or in a begrudgingly given compromise around the boardroom or in a hastily extended apology to a loved one.

They don't realize that forgiving is a verb. Too often we forget that we must live out of a forgiving heart each morning as we pull ourselves from sleep and face the day ahead. We find ourselves locked in an emotionally claustrophobic space with the walls closing in on us, overlooking the fact that we hold the key to unlock the way to safe passage. Practicing the artful actions of forgiveness requires you to unlock yourself from the shackles of unforgiveness and then extend the same freedom to those incarcerated around you.

Living in the freedom of forgiveness will sometimes require you to be innovative in its execution. As we have seen, you must extract yourself from the avalanche of anger and other reactionary emotions and focus instead on the larger design of divine designation. This process usually requires us to step back from our egos and from taking certain offenses so personally. We often must relinquish our pride and replace it with a greater sense of our purpose. Let me illustrate, literally, with an example from a friend of mine.

Soul Graffiti

A good friend of mine works in real estate and often likes to invest in rundown neighborhoods and deserted, inner-city office buildings. While he loves to be part of a movement for restoration and see a decaying, abandoned building returned to its former glory, my friend tells me that such renovations are not without unique challenges. One story in particular he shared with me made an indelible impression.

He had purchased a rundown warehouse, a former meatpacking facility, near the waterfront in downtown Chicago. The cavernous building hadn't been used in decades and would need intensive care to ensure its stability and safety as well as aesthetic attention to turn it into the suite of offices and loft apartments that my investor friend envisioned. One wall of the six-story building faced an empty parking lot that had become overgrown with weeds and cluttered with empty bottles, faded newspapers, and other debris. As the interior work on the building commenced, my friend had the exterior power-washed, scrubbed, and painted.

A week after the fledgling restoration project had been painted, looking as fresh and pristine as a white sheet on a clothesline, my friend was horrified to discover that the wall facing the parking lot had been tagged by graffiti artists. The spotless, whitewashed brick had apparently proved too tempting a canvas for the neighborhood gang to resist. At great expense, my friend had the graffiti scrubbed and the wall repainted.

However, after a week he drove up to the building to discover even more brightly colored letters and symbols sprawling across the six-story wall of his new investment. Outraged and indignant, he called the police this time, and proceeded to have the wall washed and repainted yet again. He considered hiring nighttime security but knew he could not afford the ongoing cost, especially just to prevent a group of teenagers from spray-painting the wall. You know what happened as well as I do: In less than a week, the clean wall was covered with twice as much graffiti as before.

My friend felt silly to be so upset about something that many would consider relatively trivial in the grand scheme of things. The police had filed a report but basically just shrugged their shoulders as if to indicate that it was part of the territory in the frontier of urban renovation in which he was now a trailblazer. But he refused to accept the situation as it was and tried to think through what he could do to remedy the ongoing problem. He knew tenants and residents would not feel safe if half their building was covered in gang symbols and obscenities.

Two nights later, my friend awoke in the middle of the night with either divine inspiration or the craziest idea he'd ever had—or maybe both! The next day he hired a sign painter to adorn the side of the building with a message and the owner's office number. His message was simple: NEED LOCAL ARTIST TO PAINT MURAL ON THIS WALL— SUPPLIES PROVIDED, PAYMENT NEGOTIATED BASED ON EXPERIENCE, and then his phone number. Within a couple of days, more than three dozen applicants had called to discuss the opportunity. My friend met with each one and ended up hiring not the most experienced or even most talented artists who applied, but rather the youngest and most professionally inexperienced.

He had the three young men submit a sketch of what they wanted to paint, which he approved, and then purchased the paint, sprayers, and brushes to get them started. Two weeks later the side of the building looked like something out of the Museum of Modern Art, a gigantic canvas covered with an urban abstract dreamscape of images, words, and human silhouettes. It was stunningly beautiful and immediately became the buzz of the neighborhood. In a short time, my friend had filled every vacancy and even had a waiting list of people interested in working or living in this newly adorned work of art. Impressed with the amazing job they had done with this mural, other building owners hired the three budding artists to paint other buildings in the neighborhood.

Seventy Times Seven

My friend embraced the reality of his situation and found a way to turn the tarnish of street graffiti into the sparkle of a work of art. Instead of feeding on the animosity of the situation and contributing to its cycle of infertile futility, this innovative investor stepped back and discovered a way to rethink, resee, and reapproach the offense that had been inscribed on his property. He realized that he could spend thousands of dollars scrubbing, painting and repainting, and paying for security in an attempt to control the situation and ensure that his beloved building's wall remained blank. Or he could embrace the offense as an opportunity for innovation. By releasing his anger and hostility, he could grow from it and create a lush garden out of what appeared to be an arid desert.

Almost every day, we are faced with the same challenge my friend encountered. Over our lifetime, the accumulated offenses of others will eventually begin to clutter our soul like graffiti sprayed across the walls of an abandoned building. The process of forgiveness remains an ongoing work of art that we must continue to cultivate and exercise if we are to be the vibrant, creative, balanced, effective human beings we were made to be.

Earlier in our exploration together, back in Chapter Ten, we looked at the reality of what we are actually praying when the words from the Lord's Prayer tumble from our lips: "Forgive us our trespasses as we forgive those who trespass against us." We looked at the parable of the wicked servant who begged his master for relief from the enormous debt he owed him, and upon receiving it, proceeded to torment another indebted to him for a much smaller amount without mercy. The question that precipitated this parable is one you may have heard. And the answer that Jesus initially gave to this query was so baffling for those listening that he unpacked this parable to provide vivid color to what he was saying.

With the Jewish law in mind, Peter, one of his disciples, had asked Jesus, "Lord, how many times shall I forgive my brother or sister who sins against me? Up to seven times?" (Matthew 18:21, NIV). Reinforcing the process of forgiveness through repetition was clearly the custom at that time, and seven times was deemed the standard for personal and legal restoration. However, Jesus threw everyone a curveball when he answered, "I tell you, not seven times, but seventy-seven times" (Matthew 18:22, NIV). Now, it may be tempting for some people to view his answer as a definitive, mathematical solution to the issue of forgiveness. However, as we have seen repeatedly, the way we process the wounds we incur and then hold on to them with bitterness or release them with forgiveness is not an algebra equation with clear variables and a neat, predetermined solution that you can find by flipping to the back of the textbook and checking your answer.

When Jesus tells us that we must forgive our offenders seventy-seven times, I believe he is utilizing hyperbole, the rhetorical tool of exaggeration, to make a dramatic point. And followed up by the parable of the wicked servant, his point seems quite sharply illustrated: If we truly receive the gift of God's mercy for a debt that we can never begin to pay, then our hearts will constantly practice forgiving those who hurt, offend, or infringe upon us. Forgiveness is the gift that keeps on giving. Both to you by liberating your soul from the burden of harboring so many destructive and corrosive emotions as well as to the other person by reflecting a shimmering ray of God's unconditional love to them through the way you treat them. Often the way that we keep multiplying mercy is through the actions we take to demonstrate our inner freedom.

Ready, Action!

As I have mentioned, I have been privileged to coproduce and participate in the making of several films in the past few years. It's been an eye-opening experience on many levels, but what has surprised me the most is witnessing all of the preparation that goes into shooting a scene that may only last a few minutes or even a few seconds in the final cut of the movie. You would be surprised to see how thirty seconds on the screen in the theater actually took days, sometimes weeks, to shoot.

As I have stood on set at the periphery of the scene with the director, other producers, and cast members, the process is often a great deal of hurry-up-and-wait. Everyone hustles to make sure their particular responsibilities—lighting, makeup, wardrobe, props, and so on—are as perfect as they can be so that when the director yells "Ready, action!" and the cameras are rolling they can then rest easy knowing they have done their part.

Part of the peace that comes with forgiving others, as well as being forgiven, is the confident assurance of knowing that you have done everything you can do. As we conclude our journey together within these pages, I encourage you to spend some time in prayer and reflection regarding the role you play and the actions you may need to take at this point. It may be a matter of having that hard conversation you've been putting off and simply telling someone the truth about how you feel and what forgiveness looks like.

A letter may need to be written and sent to someone who is no longer in your immediate circle of friends and acquaintances. A call made, a gift offered, even restitution provided or, if offered to you, finally accepted.

If you truly want to experience your life at the next level, then you must plunge into your unfinished business and be willing to seek out resolutions. You must be willing to take the actions that forgiveness requires and then to integrate this new freedom of spirit into your life. No, it won't be easy, but it will be infinitely more productive, satisfying, and effective than clinging to the blockage that has siphoned off your energy and preoccupied your thoughts for so long. Bitterness, anger, and resentment are poor tenants and never pay their rent. It's time to evict them from your heart and open yourself up to the clean, inviting, creative space within where you can occupy and enjoy your own life.

My friend, you must never forget to forgive. Your life depends on it! Isn't it time to unwrap the present you've been carrying around?

Acknowledgments

My passion for the message of *Let It Go* has been warmly embraced and sustained by so many people who demonstrate the power of extending and receiving forgiveness in all they do. This book is better for their contributions, for which I'm immensely grateful.

My ongoing gratitude to my publishing family at Atria Books for their passionate efforts to make this book bigger and better than any of us dreamed. I'm indebted to Judith Curr, Carolyn Reidy, Gary Urda, Yona Deshommes, Hillary Tisman, Todd Hunter, Chris Lloreda, and Lisa Keim for helping me take this much-needed message to the next level. Thank you Michael Selleck and Liz Perl for all your hard work on behalf of this project. I'm also grateful to Sue Fleming for her contribution.

I'm indebted to Malaika Adero for her insight, patience, and editorial discernment on these pages. I'm also thankful for the many times she has forgiven me for mispronouncing her name! I would like to thank Kelly Sedgwick and Regina Lewis for their research and promotions of this labor of love. Dudley Delffs shared his book wisdom and editorial expertise and helped me express my unique way with words—thank you, Dudley.

Jan Miller and Shannon Marven at Dupree Miller & Associates continue to amaze me with their tireless dedication and passionate partnership. My ongoing and abiding gratitude for all their efforts to help me get my message out with excellence, exuberance, and excitement. Jan and Shannon, I appreciate you and your team more than you know.

Any wisdom I have to share about the topic of forgiveness has been forged in the foundry of my experiences with my loving family. My beautiful wife, Serita, continues to forgive me, love me, and encourage me in ways that reflect the grace of God every day. My children have taught me what it means to forgive and to be forgiven in ways I never expected. Thank you for providing me with the comfort and shelter of your love, for letting go of offenses, and holding tight to the joys we share.